Successful Grant Writing

Laura N. Gitlin, PhD, is Associate Professor in the Department of Occupational Therapy and Director of Research in the Center for Collaborative Research in the College of Allied Health Sciences at Thomas Jefferson University, in Philadelphia. As part of her responsibilities, she engages in federal and foundation grant development and writing and in developing grant management systems. Dr. Gitlin is a funded researcher, having received research and training grants from both federal agencies and private foundations, including the National Institute on Disability and Rehabilitation Research and the National Institute on Aging. She has served on peer review panels for the National Institute on Disability and Rehabilitation Research, the Agency for Health Care Policy and Research, and the American Occupational Therapy Foundation. She has published extensively in peer-reviewed journals and is a coauthor of a book on quantitative and qualitative research methodologies.

Kevin J. Lyons, PhD, directs the Center for Collaborative Research in the College of Allied Health Sciences at Thomas Jefferson University, in Philadelphia. He is also Associate Dean in both the College of Allied Health Sciences and the College of Graduate Studies, where he oversees nursing and allied health graduate programs. Dr. Lyons holds academic appointments in the Department of General Studies and the Department of Occupational Therapy and teaches graduate courses in research design, leadership, and management. Dr. Lyons has been active in research development on a national level. He serves on peer review panels for the National Institute on Disability and Rehabilitation Research and the Bureau of Health Professions, and reviews proposals for the American Educational Research Association and the American Evaluation Society. He received the J. Warren Perry Distinguished Author Award from the Association of Schools of Allied Health Professions and has been elected a Fellow in that organization.

SUCCESSFUL GRANT WRITING

Strategies for Health and Human Service Professionals

LAURA N. GITLIN, PhD

KEVIN J. LYONS, PhD

SPRINGER PUBLISHING COMPANY

Springer Publishing Company, Inc.
536 Broadway
New York, NY 10012-3955

Cover design by Tom Yabut
Production Editor: Pamela Ritzer

00 01 02 / 6 5 4   Fourth Printing

Library of Congress Cataloging-in-Publication Data

Gitlin, Laura N., 1952–
    Successful grant writing: Strategies for health and human service professionals / Laura N. Gitlin and Kevin J. Lyons.
        p.   cm.
    Includes bibliographical references and index.
    ISBN 0-8261-9260-2
    1. Proposal writing in human services.   2. Medical care—Research grants.   3. Public health—Research grants.   4. Proposal writing for grants.   I. Lyons, Kevin J.   II. Title.
HV41.2.G58   1996
361'.0068'1—dc20   95-46547
                                                    CIP

Printed in the United States of America

To Eduardo, Keith, and Eric,
siempre en mi corazon y mente.

LNG

To Brendan, Margaret, Patrick, and Bridget,
There is no greater inspiration than that
which comes from love.

KJL

To our colleagues whose creative ideas and
dedication to the improvement
of health care for all makes grantsmanship
worthwhile.

Contents

Preface

There are many books, pamphlets, and newsletters on writing competitive grant applications. Few however, address the topic from the perspective of the health and human service professional. *Successful Grant Writing: Strategies for Health and Human Services Professionals* is specially designed for health and human service professionals and is written for those in academic and practice settings who are either inexperienced grant writers or who have had some success but would like to expand their knowledge of the process and become more systematic in obtaining external support.

The health and human service professions are at the crossroads of significant transformation and redefinition. Obtaining external funding to examine professional issues, improve services, or develop and test new education, service, and research models is rapidly becoming an essential of professional life. This book, therefore, includes a range of strategies and work models that are appropriate for professionals who have different growth needs and opportunities for funding. It is our hope that it will contribute to the transformation of health care by providing a framework for understanding the funding world and offering definitive and effective strategies for success in this environment.

HOW TO USE THIS BOOK

This book moves the reader from an understanding of the language and basic components of grantsmanship in Part I to developing your own ideas for funding in Part II, writing the sections of a proposal in Part III, organizing different types of project structures in Part IV, and finally, to understanding the review process in Part V. Each chapter describes a specific aspect of grantsmanship and suggests innovative strategies by which to implement the information that is presented. These strategies may be beneficial to individuals or departments in academic, clinical, or community-based settings. They can be used by an individual to outline a course of action to pursue independent grant activity or by a department to plan a systematic approach to capturing external funding. The appendixes contain helpful materials, such as a list of key acronyms, examples of time lines, and sample budget sheets.

The guidelines and suggestions in this book are based on mor e than 13 years of experience by the authors in obtaining external support for education and research programs and in working with individuals in the health and human services, as well as from the analyses of interviews with experienced grant writers and program officers in key federal and other government agencies and foundations.

Acknowledgments

The development of a portion of the materials for this book was supported by a contract from the Bureau of Health Professions, Health Resources and Services Administration, Public Health Service [purchase order # HRSA 92-850(P)]. We gratefully acknowledge the assistance of Captain Fred G. Paavola, Dr. Marcia K. Brand, and Dr. Norman L. Clark of the Bureau of Health Professions for their support and belief in the importance of this project. We greatly benefited from interviewing Drs. Don Blodgett and Martha Bokee, Department of Education; and Dr. Linda Siegenthaler, Agency for Health Care Policy and Research. We also thank Dr. Maralynne D. Mitcham and Becki Trickey of the Medical University of South Carolina and Dr. Christopher A. Squier of the University of Iowa for their careful review and insightful comments. Special thanks go to Ms. Lisa Marzucco for her invaluable assistance in organizing, formatting, and proofreading manuscript drafts. The opinions expressed in this book, however, are those of the authors and should not be construed to represent the opinions of any federal agency, foundation, program officer, or other individual.

Introduction

You have a great idea that you believe can significantly improve the educational program for your students or services to your clients. To carry out the idea you probably will require financial support. How can you obtain this support?

One way is to apply for a grant from the federal government, a private foundation, or a corporation. A grant is a mechanism by which an agency awards money to conduct a research study or other activity, such as an educational program, service activity, demonstration, or research project.

The task of writing a grant proposal, or even knowing how to get started can be daunting, especially if it is your first attempt. As with any venture, grantsmanship has a language of its own, a set of rules, and relatively standard procedures, all of which you can learn and become successful in using.

But you may well ask why you need to learn the process of grantsmanship. After all, it involves considerable time and effort and the need to learn a new set of skills. There is more than one purpose for getting a grant. Obviously, if you need money to develop and implement a new program, a grant is one way to obtain that support. However, there are other very important but less tangible reasons to pursue external funding.

What can grants do for you?

Grants can:

- Develop and advance knowledge in a field.
- Support training and research activities.

- Provide institutional support.
- Expand opportunities for student/clinician education.
- Legitimize research or training projects.
- Enhance institutional prestige.
- Promote individual advancement.

Let's examine each of these reasons more closely.

Develop and advance knowledge in a field: The basic mission of most federal funding agencies and the reason those in the health and human service professions pursue a research or educational grant is to develop and advance knowledge in a particular field. For example, funding for a research study on the determinants of older women's compliance with mammography or for examining the impact of a home intervention to help frail elders is critical for advancing knowledge in these areas and improving the health and functioning of individuals and groups. The support for model educational programs also leads to new and effective instructional methods that can improve the practice of health and human service professionals.

Support training and research activities: Another purpose of grant funding is to support the development and implementation of new training programs. Developing new programs can be expensive, and institutions are often hesitant to support new ventures unless they have been systematically tested and shown to be effective. Training or education grants can be important catalysts for implementing change in an institution's approach to educating health and human service professionals.

Provide institutional support: Success in gaining external funding can also contribute to the vitality and financial health of your department, school, or agency. The direct costs derived from a funded project may support a special program your agency wants to run or, in some cases, contribute toward its general operating expenses. At a university funds might pay for part of your salary or other important staff members as well as support such services as secretarial assistance or consultants and expenses like professional travel. The indirect cost recovery, which is defined later in this book, helps defray operating costs such as heat, light, and telephone use.

Expand opportunities for student/clinician education: As college tuition continues to rise, it becomes increasingly difficult for students to afford an education, particularly in the health and human service fields, where salaries are rarely adequate to offset these costs. Many PhD students in the basic biomedical sciences are often fully or partially supported by funded research projects. Similar opportunities are available in many of the health and human service fields, primarily through the support of positions such as research assistants, interviewers, or project coordinators.

Legitimize research or training projects: Obtaining funding for your project is public recognition of the worth of your educational or research program. Grant applications are reviewed and approved by a jury of your peers, and this process provides external validation and legitimation of your research or educational plan. An award indicates that experts in the field acknowledge your idea as important and worthy of public or private support.

Enhance institutional prestige: Health and human service professionals in higher education are increasingly encouraged to obtain external funding, not only to advance knowledge in their field but also to contribute to the prestige of their institution. External funding is often used as an index of the prestige of a college or university and the quality of its faculty. As a result, many universities measure quality, in part, by the extent to which faculty members obtain external funding. It is no longer true that schools or departments educating health and human service professionals will be recognized as contributing to the institution only through its training of competent clinicians. These schools are now being evaluated on their contribution to the overall research mission of the university. In some cases, their continuation in the institution is dependent on the extent to which the research mission is actively pursued.

Promote individual advancement: A funded grant also enhances the professional standing of an individual, both within the institution and in the profession at large. Funded health professionals become known among their peers through professional newsletters, journals, or other national forums and valued for their skills. Thus, funding success not only advances your knowledge base and professional development but will also provide increased professional prestige and job mobility.

Part I

The Perspective of Funding Agencies

Welcome to the world of grantsmanship! Grantsmanship is the process of using knowledge and implementing a series of activities from which to obtain a grant to carry out a program. It is both an art and technical skill that involves lots of hard work, a "state of readiness," and sometimes trial and error prior to a successful outcome.

A basic tenet of successful grantsmanship is to be well informed and, above all else, to know the source from which funds are being sought. The more you know about a funding agency, the greater the likelihood that you will be able to write a proposal that is tailor made to fit the intent and priorities of the funding source.

The funding environment is in constant change. This is especially true today in light of the health care reform movement and government cut-backs in funding. Therefore, finding the right funder for your particular idea can take time and require knowledge of multiple sources that provide information about funding opportunities. We therefore begin in chapter 1 by describing the perspective of funding agencies and introducing the language that this world uses. We then examine, in chapter 2, the sources from which to learn about funding opportunities and how to interpret their messages to you.

Chapter 1

Getting Started

Do you have a great idea but need money to carry it out? If you do, then who will pay for it? Where can you obtain information about sources for support? What is the best way to persuade a funding source to support your idea?

These are questions that many health and human service professionals ask. Fortunately, there are agencies in both the public and private sector who have money to give to worthy projects. Your job is first to find out where and how to look for pockets of money and then learn how to write a grant application to convince a funding agency that your project is important. This is the essence of grantsmanship.

The first point to understand about grantsmanship is that you are not competing with a funding agency. Most people do not realize that a purpose of federal funding agencies and private foundations is to give money away. Consider, for example, agencies of the federal government that are funded by Congress to solve problems facing the American people. Each agency is charged with the responsibility of addressing a different issue, such as women's health or cancer prevention. Based on its charge, the agency sets priorities for the types of grant programs to fund. Each year these agencies have to compete for funds from Congress to support their grant programs. To obtain congressional funds, an agency may demonstrate to Congress the significant progress that is being made in addressing a problem area. One indication of progress is the quality of the grant programs that are funded and the contributions that these programs have made to the advancement of knowledge and practice. Therefore, it is in an agency's best interest to encourage the submission and approval of as many good proposals as possible.

How do inexperienced investigators compete for this funding? The process is not very complicated, but there are specific rules and strategies that you need to learn if you are to be successful. To illustrate this point, let's look at a typical situation.

A GRANT STORY

Ms. L. is an assistant professor of social work at an urban university. The school in which she works has departments of physical therapy, occupational therapy, and nursing. Ms. L. volunteers in a number of homeless shelters throughout the city and has organized a student volunteer program. In her volunteer work she notices that shelter residents have significant health problems and difficulties accessing social services. She is convinced that a formal educational program to prepare social work, nursing, and allied health students to work in these shelters is essential to help alleviate some of these problems. Unfortunately, she does not know how to go about organizing such a program.

Ms. L. decides to meet with her department chairman to inquire about enrolling more students into the shelters and to suggest that the department offer a formal educational program. At the meeting her chairman points out that, although Ms. L.'s idea is good, starting a new program is expensive and time-consuming. Because the school is short of both money and faculty, the chairman tells her that it is not possible to put the department's limited resources into her program idea. The only way that such a program could be supported would be for Ms. L. to find money elsewhere to pay for its development and implementation.

During her next evening of volunteer work, Ms. L. becomes even more determined to do something about the health problems she sees. The next day she makes an appointment to meet with a senior faculty member, Dr. A., who has received grant funding for a number of projects. She explains her idea and asks for advice. Dr. A. is sympathetic but tells her that because of her inexperience she will have to be patient and develop a systematic plan to pursue funding. He suggests casting a wide net in searching for a funding agency, because her inexperience will make it difficult to obtain funding from the larger, well-known federal agencies such as the National Institutes of Health (NIH). He also suggests that she work with others who are more experienced grant writers. These people would not only help her gain experience, but their participation on her grant team would enhance her idea and make it more competitive.

Ms. L. then meets individually with senior faculty members in the departments of nursing, occupational therapy, and physical therapy. She explains the problems she has seen in the homeless shelters and asks if they would be interested in helping her write a grant proposal to develop an educational program to prepare students to work in the shelters. All of the faculty members express great enthusiasm and suggest that Ms. L. call a meeting once she has identified potential funding sources. Ms. L. agrees and sets out to do her homework.

Where does Ms. L. begin in her search for funding? Her first step would be to learn the language of grantsmanship.

THE LANGUAGE OF GRANTSMANSHIP

As in other fields of endeavor, there is a specific language that is common to grantsmanship. It is important to learn this language in order to understand the grant writing process, communicate with agency personnel, and interpret application instructions for submitting a proposal idea. In the following sections, 14 terms that are commonly used in the funding environment and throughout this book are defined and will get you started in understanding agency language and communicating with those in this environment.

Research Grants

Research grants provide money for an investigator to conduct a specific area of scientific inquiry, either basic or applied. In basic research, an investigator examines a question that will add to the theoretical body of knowledge in a discipline. In applied research, the investigator applies a specific theoretical principle, program, or approach to a practical situation. A research grant will usually provide money for salary support of the investigator and his or her team, materials needed to carry out the research (laboratory specimens, chemicals, supplies, mailings), data analysis, and travel to professional meetings. A research grant also may provide stipends for graduate or undergraduate students. In some instances the grant will pay for the purchase of special equipment needed to carry out the project.

Training or Educational Grants

Training or educational grants are those that have as a main purpose the education or training of students, faculty, clinicians, or other practitioners. These grants are used for planning and implementing new undergraduate or graduate programs, revising or updating curriculum materials, recruiting students into special programs, or helping health and human service professionals gain new knowledge or develop new skills. They also provide money for salary, supplies, travel, consultants, graduate students, and, in some instances, equipment. One difference between training grants and research grants is that training grants will often provide money for student tuition and/or stipends and living expenses.

Demonstration Grants

Demonstration grants provide support to projects that evaluate a model program, set of services, or methodology. A demonstration project usually builds on existing knowledge that suggests that a given model or service is an effective way to address a specific issue. These types of grants are most commonly pursued by health and human service providers who wish to expand existing services or develop innovative model programs that can be replicated.

Agency

The term *agency* will be used throughout this manual to refer to any funding source. The reason for using the more generic term is that most funding agencies have a variety of departments that are called by different names. For example, the federal government is divided into a bewildering array of organizational units called centers, offices, institutes, bureaus, divisions, departments, or administrations, all of which may have programs of funding. Private foundations have different organizational structures through which money is awarded. Private companies also have their own way of naming departments that provide support for projects.

Call for Proposals

A call for proposals is a notice of an opportunity to submit a proposal on a specific topic. These announcements vary considerably in how specific they are in describing the projects they would like to see submitted. The federal government tends to provide very detailed descriptions of what needs to be included in grant proposals. Foundations and private companies tend to be much more general. These types of calls for proposals are referred to as requests for applications (RFA). Agencies often specify a particular problem that they want investigated and publish an announcement inviting interested parties to propose how they would investigate this problem.

Competition

The term *competition* will be used throughout this manual. It simply refers to a particular grant program for which a call for competitive proposals has been issued.

Preferences, Priorities, and Special Considerations

Frequently, a federal agency will prefer to fund proposals that give attention to a specific issue related to the general topic they want addressed. For example, many agencies are interested in projects that are interdisciplinary in nature or that are focused on underserved populations. When this is the case, they will indicate in the call for proposals that "extra credit" will be given to proposals that include attention to these approaches. There are three categories for which extra credit may be given: funding preferences, funding priorities, and special considerations.

In competitions with a *funding preference,* special attention is given to applications that fit the stated preference. For example, if your proposal meets the basic requirements for approval *and* for the funding preference, you will usually be funded before applicants who have been approved for funding but who did not meet the preference qualification. If you qualify for a *funding priority,* the score assigned to your proposal will usually be adjusted favorably by a predetermined numeric value, such as 5 or 10 points. In competitions that include a *special consideration,* each reviewer has additional latitude in assigning points to your proposal score. Each agency decides whether or not to use one or more of these funding mechanisms, although in some instances one of them is required by the authorizing legislation for that particular grant program. If one or more of these mechanisms is offered, you should seriously consider trying to qualify. Although not required for approval, it will make your application more competitive. Be sure to state in your proposal that you are requesting a preference, priority, or special consideration and describe the specific reasons why.

Program Guide or General Instructions

The program guide (sometimes called general instructions) provides general information about a particular grant program. It presents information about the purpose of the grant program, definitions of important terms, application procedures, eligibility requirements, the review process and evaluation criteria, information about funding priorities, preferences and special considerations, and other guidelines to help you write your proposal. The program guide should be read very carefully because it not only contains information to help structure your proposal, but also requirements that must be followed.

Supplemental Instructions

Supplemental instructions extend or modify the program guide. These instructions also contain changes to the guide that are specific to a particular competition. They are updated annually and duplicate some of the information found in the program guide and additional details, such as the required number of proposal copies; individuals to contact for information; additional definitions that are pertinent to a specific competition; and a more detailed description of the content of each section of the application and the funding priorities, preferences, and special considerations. Read these instructions carefully. If significant changes have been made after the program guide has been printed, your application may suffer competitively if the supplemental instructions are not followed.

Grantee/Grantor

The grantee is the institution or individual who submits the grant application and receives a grant award. A grantor is the agency providing the grant funds.

Principal Investigator/Project Director

The principal investigator is the person who will direct a grant project. This title is used most often in research grants. A project director is the term applied to the person directing a training, educational, or demonstration grant. In both cases, this is the person who oversees the grant activity, assures the scientific integrity of the endeavor, and is responsible for assuring that the grant is conducted in accordance with all conditions and federal regulations.

Program Officer/Project Officer

A program officer is an employee of a federal agency who manages a specific program of grant funding. Foundations also use program officers to oversee their competitions. A project officer is someone who is assigned to supervise and provide technical assistance to a particular funded grant.

Peer Review Panel

A peer review panel is a group of experts selected by an agency to evaluate grant proposals submitted in response to a call for proposals. The panel evaluates each proposal and makes recommendations to the agency as to which should be funded. Each agency may use and structure panels in different ways. The structure and composition of panels within the federal government are determined by statute or other federal guidelines. The National Institutes of Health, for example, select individuals who represent different knowledge areas, such as health services, behavioral science, or medical research. These panels are called initial review groups (IRGs) or study sections. Members are appointed for specified periods of time (usually 3 years) and usually meet 3 times a year to review proposals. Other agencies may select panels for one particular competition. Panels may vary in size from 3 to perhaps 15 experts. A number of different formats are used when convening review panels. This is discussed further in chapter 11.

Many private foundations do not use peer review panels. Decisions regarding funding are made by the board of directors or trustees of the foundation, often based on the evaluation and recommendations made by program officers who work for the foundation. Proposals may also be reviewed by foundation work groups or committees of experts who are convened for a specific competition.

Pink Sheets

"Pink sheets" are written evaluations of proposals that are sent to the principal investigators or program directors. They are named, quite simply, for the color of the paper on which they are often printed. The pink sheet usually provides an in-depth narrative assessment of a proposal, including an overall summary of the strengths and weaknesses, the panel's critique of each section, and recommendations or suggestions for improvement. Careful attention to this critique is important because it can provide an indication of whether or not it is appropriate to revise your application and resubmit at another time if necessary.

Funding Cycle

Most federal competitions follow a funding cycle; this refers to the due date of applications up to the time awards are made. Many federal agencies have funding cycles that occur at the same time each year. For example, in the NIH system, there are three submission deadlines for submitting individual investigator research grant applications (commonly referred to as an RO-1 award): October 1, February 1, and June 1. When inquiring about a particular grant program, always ask when proposals are due and the anticipated time of award.

Chapter 2

Becoming Familiar with Funding Sources

N ow that Ms. L. has become familiar with the language of grants-manship, her next step is to learn about potential sources of funding for her idea. Although identifying an idea for a project is important, even the greatest idea will not be funded if it does not match the interest of an agency. Therefore, it is important to develop a plan by which to learn about the types of projects various agencies want to support. Because the funding environment and the interests of agencies are constantly evolving, it is also important to monitor changes in agency policies. A plan of action is particularly important if your idea is in a formative stage. Keep in mind that once a notice or call for proposals reaches a public source such as the *Federal Register,* you may have only 6 weeks in which to develop a proposal. Proposal writing can be very time-consuming, and 6 weeks may not be suffi-cient to develop a project idea and write a proposal that will be com-petitive. In this chapter we identify the major sources of funding for health and human service professionals, discuss ways to learn about the current and future interests of various funding agencies, and sug-gest how to interpret the agency's call for proposals.

SOURCES OF FUNDING FOR HEALTH
AND HUMAN SERVICE PROFESSIONS

There are four major sources of grant funding for health and human service projects: the federal government, private foundations, professional organizations, and private industry.

These four sources, discussed below, offer opportunities for funding a range of projects, such as small pilot research, conferences, and demonstration projects or large-scale education or research programs. In searching for funding, it is initially wise to cast a wide net. There are pockets of money available, often in seemingly unlikely agencies. Let's examine each of these four sources.

Federal Government

The federal government is a huge enterprise composed of an array of departments, agencies, institutes, bureaus, and centers. Its complex bureaucracy can make it difficult for inexperienced investigators to navigate their way through this federal maze. Further complicating the situation is the dynamic nature of the funding environment. The priorities and interests of the various agencies are always changing in response to advances in knowledge, societal trends, and congressional activity. The federal government is, however, still the largest source of research and training money. The National Institutes of Health alone have a budget of approximately $11 billion!

As you search for funding among the federal agencies, you will find that some may have interests that are generally similar to yours. If you search intelligently, you may also be able to identify agencies that initially appear unlikely to fund your ideas but that may prove important to pursue in the long run. For example, it is not uncommon for legislators to direct money for education or social services programs that benefit their constituents to federal agencies not usually associated with human services. These "pork barrel" projects are very common. The *Washington Post* reported on March 28, 1995, that the $243 billion defense appropriation, passed the previous year, contained numerous nondefense programs, such as a $10 million National Guard program to help Los Angeles youth and another $1.5 million to round up wild horses wandering onto the White Sands Missile Range. Agencies may also receive money for programs of particular interest or value to their employees. Again, the Department of Defense, which provides a variety of training programs for its employees, recently received $210 million for studies on breast cancer. Similarly, the Department of Agriculture has had money in the past to fund many projects that one might expect to find in the Department of Education.

Although there may be pockets of money for health and human service professionals throughout the federal government, there are two departments in particular that contain agencies with a focused interest in health and human service areas. These are the Public Health Service (in the Department of Health and Human Services) and the Department of Education. Within the Department of Education, the Office of Special Education and Rehabilitation Services (OSERS) has a variety of programs of potential interest to the health professions, as does the National Institute on Disability and Rehabilitation Research (NIDRR). The Fund for the Improvement of Post-Secondary Education (FIPSE), which is a foundation within the Department of Education, has many competitions that require innovative and generalizable approaches to educational problems.

Private Foundations

Private foundations are also excellent sources of funding for human service projects. There are more than 26,000 foundations in the United States that offer grants to individuals, institutions, and other nonprofit groups. These foundations hold assets of over $150 billion and award over $8 billion a year in grants.

According to the *Foundation Directory,* foundations can be categorized into four types: independent foundations, company-sponsored foundations, operating foundations, and community foundations. Generally, only the first two types provide grants to independent investigators, although all four offer potential funding opportunities.

1. *Independent foundations* have as their primary function the awarding of grants. The assets of most of these foundations are derived from gifts of individuals or families. Some operate under the direction of family members, whereas others are under the direction of a board of trustees. A board of trustees usually ensures that funds are spent for grant programs that were intended by the family. Still other foundations function more independently in awarding grants. The Pew Charitable

Trusts and the Rockefeller Foundation are examples of two of the largest independent foundations. There are hundreds of other smaller foundations that also fund projects relevant to health and human service providers.

2. *Company-sponsored foundations* have derived their funds from a profit-making company or corporation. They generally, but not always, award grants that are related to the business interest of the parent corporation. Two examples of these foundations are the Anheuser-Busch and Kellogg Foundations.

3. *Operating foundations* support research, social welfare, or other programs determined by their governing body. These foundations rarely award grants to outside organizations.

4. *Community foundations* are those whose funds are derived from many donors. These are often classified as public charities and generally limit their giving to charitable organizations in the local community.

Professional Organizations

Your professional association is another appropriate source of funding. It is particularly useful for beginning investigators because the interest of such an association is to support the professional development of its members and to conduct projects to advance the profession. Many associations provide small grants that can range from $2,000 to $30,000.

Drug Companies and Private Industry

Drug companies, equipment manufacturers, and other companies related to health care often have money available for small projects. Many large corporations have funds for research projects that advance the interests of the company. The main interest of companies in the private sector is testing or evaluating their own products. For example, an oral health care company may need a new product tested for the prevention of plaque, an equipment manufacturer may need a new assistive device evaluated, or a company may pay for the development of a patient education video that promotes its product. The private sector is an untapped potential source of funding.

LEARNING ABOUT AND KEEPING TRACK OF FUNDING SOURCES

In searching for funding, look for sources of support in both obvious and unlikely places. But where can you learn about funding opportunities? Here we describe 21 common sources used by investigators to learn about funding interests in the public and private sectors, including those that are specific to the federal level, those that pertain to foundations and corporations, and those that are related to professional associations. If you are unsure of which agencies support your areas of interest, develop a search strategy that includes as many of these sources as possible.

Federal Government

Program Officers

Perhaps the most valuable sources of information about funding are program officers in federal agencies. These individuals can provide invaluable assistance at all stages of the grant development process. Program officers usually have extensive experience overseeing grant competitions, know the type of project that will be most competitive in their agency, and can give you valuable suggestions about how to shape your idea to fit the requirements of a particular competition. In some cases, a program officer may have responsibility in the development of the call for proposals and therefore will be able to provide specific advice about the type of project the agency would like to see funded. Before you make a commitment to pursue a particular project, *call a program officer.* The name and telephone number of a program officer can be found in calls for proposals in the *Federal Register* and the *NIH Guide.* Often, the suggestions and advice a program officer provides can result in the submission of a stronger proposal.

Beginning investigators are often hesitant to contact a government official. However, program officers welcome calls and visits. Table 2.1 contains suggestions about what to say when contacting a program officer by telephone.

When you talk to a program officer, identify yourself, briefly explain your idea, and ask if his or her agency might be interested in funding a proposal based on this idea. Also ask whether you can mail or fax a one- or two-page description of your project. In many agencies,

TABLE 2.1   What to Say to a Program Officer by Telephone

1. State your name.
2. Give the name of your institution.
3. Describe your general idea and indicate the strengths you would bring to bear to a project.
4. Ask if the agency supports a program on the topic area.
5. Request an application kit and funding deadline.
6. Ask if the program officer is able to review an abstract, concept paper, or draft of a grant application prior to submission.
7. Ask if you can review proposals that have been funded in a prior competition if you decide to visit Washington.

a program officer will review this abstract or concept paper and inform you as to whether it would be appropriate to submit a proposal. If your idea does not fit the goals of the agency, the program officer will let you know this as well and might be able to suggest a more appropriate agency.

You can also visit program officers in Washington, DC. Unless an agency is in the middle of a peer review, you will usually be able to obtain an appointment. Table 2.2 presents seven suggestions to help you plan and conduct a visit with a program officer.

When you visit a program officer, plan for a 30–45-minute meeting. Before the meeting, learn about the kinds of projects the agency has funded in the past and its current areas of interest. The ways in which you can obtain this information are discussed later in this chapter. At the meeting, do not be reluctant to ask very basic questions, such as what the agency looks for in a grant proposal, how the peer review process works, and/or what competitions are upcoming. You will find that program officers are not only very helpful, patient, and pleasant, but very candid about what you need to do to be successful. If you plan carefully, you may be able to visit three or four program officers in one day.

Main Information Number of a Federal Agency

Let's say you are unsure which program officer in a particular agency would be most helpful for your idea. You can call the main number of an agency and describe your idea in nontechnical terms; the secretary will be able to direct your request to the most appropriate individual.

TABLE 2.2 Visiting a Program Officer

Before visit:
1. Review application materials and legislative priorities.
2. Learn what kinds of projects the agency usually funds.
3. Learn what the agency has funded in the past 2 years.

What to ask during the visit:
1. What are the common strengths and weaknesses of proposals submitted to your agency?
2. What are the major areas that will be emphasized by the agency in the current funding cycle?
3. What are the anticipated future areas of interest to the agency?
4. Can proposals that have been funded by the agency in the past be reviewed?

Catalog of Federal Domestic Assistance

Another important source of funding information is published once a year and contains a listing of funding sources in the federal government. Each entry includes the title of a program, the name of the contact person, a brief summary of the kinds of projects that are funded, the amount of money available, the average size of awards, and whether a funding cycle is anticipated during the upcoming year.

Monitoring Legislation and Government Documents

Monitoring the progress of major legislation is an important way of anticipating future funding initiatives. Congress appropriates money to all federal agencies with a general expectation that it will be used to investigate concerns of importance to the American people. For example, public concern regarding diseases such as AIDS and cancer have resulted in effective lobbying efforts on the part of special interest groups to support more research on these diseases. Congress has responded positively to this pressure and has earmarked increasing amounts of money to address these problems. Because federal agencies must compete for funds, they often structure their planning agenda around issues of congressional importance. For example, some institutes in the NIH have received increased levels of funding for basic research in cancer and AIDS. Agencies that do not specialize in basic research may approach the problem of AIDS from a different perspective. For example, the Department of Education has an interest in funding AIDS education programs in the public schools.

One way to monitor legislation is to contact your senator or representative. When you visit Washington, DC, make an appointment to discuss your interests and to learn about the legislative agenda of your congressperson. Appointments with legislative aides, who have detailed knowledge of the major issues on Capitol Hill, are usually easy to obtain.

You may also contact the government affairs office of your professional association. Members of this group will be monitoring legislation important to your profession and may be lobbying for a specific program of interest. They will also be very knowledgeable about upcoming legislative issues.

Congressional Offices

Your congressional representative can also help you locate appropriate funding sources. Write a letter to your senator or congressperson, explaining the nature of your idea and asking for assistance in locating an appropriate government source of support. The congressperson's aide for health legislation will review your letter, label it "controlled correspondence," and forward it to one or more appropriate agencies. These agencies will then respond with suggestions. When writing to your congressperson, highlight how your proposed project may potentially benefit people in his or her congressional district.

Federal Register

The *Federal Register* is a daily (Monday through Friday) publication of the federal government. It provides a public announcement of regulations and legal notices issued by federal agencies, such as presidential proclamations, executive orders, federal agency documents that have general applicability and legal effect, documents required to be published by acts of Congress, and other documents of public interest. All calls for proposals are listed in this publication; therefore, reading it will help you learn what agencies are funding programs in your area of interest. The office of the *Federal Register* often conducts public workshops that describe what the *Federal Register* is and how to use it. Information regarding these workshops is published periodically on page II. Subscriptions are available for approximately $400/year. To obtain a subscription, write to New Orders, Superintendent of Documents, P.O. Box 371954, Pittsburgh, PA 15250-7954.

Notices of Upcoming Competitions Published for Comments

Prior to issuing a call for proposals for a major new competition, an announcement is printed in the *Federal Register* that invites anyone to comment about the scope and substance of the proposed competition. These announcements indicate that there will be an upcoming call for proposals in the area for which comments are sought. Anyone can respond in writing to the proposed priorities or suggest ways to improve the announcement. The agency evaluates each comment and responds to them in later editions of the *Federal Register.* The final program announcement may be altered on the basis of these comments. However, any changes will usually be minor, and the final announcement will be similar to that which is finally published as a call for proposals. Therefore, reviewing these notices provides an opportunity for you to plan ahead and begin developing your proposal idea.

Health Care Grants and Contracts Weekly

For those of you who do not have access to the daily *Federal Register,* an alternative source is the *Health Care Grants and Contracts Weekly,* a 10-page newsletter that summarizes upcoming grant competitions that are appropriate for health care professionals. It also contains information about new federal or foundation programs. The price is $320/year. For a subscription, write to Capitol Publications, Inc., P.O. Box 1453, Alexandria, VA 22313-2053. The company also publishes newsletters devoted to funding opportunities in other disciplines, such as education.

NIH Guide

The *NIH Guide* is a weekly publication of the NIH Public Health Service that announces upcoming grant and contract opportunities. It also provides policy and administrative information such as requirements and changes in extramural programs administered by the NIH. Similar information is published in the *Federal Register,* but the *NIH Guide* provides a more focused look at this group of funding agencies. It can be obtained by writing to the Printing and Reproduction Branch, National Institutes of Health, Room B4BN23, Building 31, Bethesda, MD 20892. It is also available electronically via Bitnet or Internet or through the NIH Grant Line, using a personal computer.

Commerce Business Daily (CBD)

The *CBD* is a daily publication announcing federal grant and contract opportunities. Federal agencies, by law, must advertise contracts worth $25,000 or more in the *CBD* first. Referred to as the "federal government's official want ads," the *CBD* has as its primary mission publication of requests for proposals. In the past, the *CBD* was predominantly used to solicit contracts. However, more recently, agencies are using it to attract grant proposals as well. This publication is very comprehensive in that it publishes over half a million solicitations, worth over $200 billion, each year. Your library or office of research administration may have the most up-to-date copies of the *CBD*.

Because the *CBD* is so comprehensive, it can be very difficult to review. A second option is to subscribe to a weekly summary, called the *Commerce Business Daily Weekly Release*. This publication is a customized summary of solicitations published in the preceding week. You may select certain areas, such as education, health care, or clinical research, and receive a customized listing of solicitations in these areas. This summary is available from United Communications Group, 1300 Rockville Pike, Suite 1100, Rockville, MD 20852-3030.

Although contracts can be a source of funding for health professionals, the application process and the technical requirements are different from those for grants, and discussion of them is beyond the scope of this book. For information, contact Commerce Business Daily, Commerce Department, Washington, DC 20230, (202) 482-0732. For subscription information, contact the Superintendent of Documents, Washington, DC 20402-9238, (202) 783-3238.

Serving on Peer Review Panels

Agencies frequently try to identify qualified professionals to serve on peer review panels. Serving as a peer reviewer is an invaluable experience in that it provides a great opportunity to learn about the characteristics of successful and unsuccessful grants and to enhance your skills at grantsmanship. The process of becoming a peer reviewer differs in each agency. In some agencies, particularly those within the Department of Education, you can submit your curriculum vitae with a letter requesting consideration for service on a peer review panel. In your letter, clearly identify your areas of expertise and the types of applications you believe you are qualified to review. The agencies usually will send you a data form to complete, which they then keep on file. Being selected to serve as a peer reviewer is an honor and indicates that you are recognized as a leader or major contributor in your field. A program officer in any agency can inform you as to how to be considered for service on a peer review panel.

Serving on Agency Planning Groups

Agencies often convene planning meetings with their funded investigators. These meetings are designed to identify the current state of knowledge in a field and to recommend new research or educational directions for the agency. Opportunities to serve on planning groups are usually reserved for individuals who have been previously funded by an agency. Once you are funded, ask your project officer about such opportunities. Often an agency will publish proceedings from planning meetings and make these documents available. They can be very valuable sources of information because they provide a general long-range plan for the agency.

Foundations and Corporations

Foundations and corporations are another source of potential funding for health and human service professionals. With the anticipated and real cuts in federal spending, these funding sources are increasingly receiving attention by those who formerly have been well supported by federal funds.

Foundation Directory

If you are interested in pursuing funding from private foundations, the best source of information is the *Foundation Directory,* which lists foundations that hold assets of at least $2 million or give at least $200,000 per year in grants. The latest edition (No. 15) includes information on over 6,300 foundations. Each entry includes the name and address of the foundation, a description of its general funding interests, a list of officers and trustees, the types of grants and other forms of support they award, restrictions on their programs by geographic location and subject area, and application procedures. Although foundations do fund research projects, many are also interested in demonstration projects or projects that test a model program so that it can be replicated at other sites. Most university libraries have the latest edition of the *Foundation Directory.*

Large foundations, such as the Robert Wood Johnson Foundation or the Kellogg Foundation, often fund medical and health-related projects. However, these foundations tend to fund experienced researchers or those that have received funding before. A good source for the inexperienced investigator is the smaller foundation that offers funds for pilot efforts or small projects in health care.

To help identify smaller foundations, use a second directory called the *Foundation Directory Part 2.* It contains information on mid-size foundations that give between $50,000 and $200,000 yearly. The current edition of this publication contains a listing of over 4,300 such foundations.

Both directories can be ordered from The Foundation Center, 79 Fifth Avenue, New York, NY, 10003-3076.

Foundation Annual Reports and Newsletters

An excellent supplement to the *Foundation Directory* is the annual report of a foundation. The annual report provides detailed information on projects supported during the past year. Past project funding is one of the best indications of the current interests of the foundation. Many also publish newsletters that describe ongoing projects and announce upcoming initiatives. To learn more about these opportunities, write or call a foundation and ask that your name be put on its mailing list.

Annual Reports of Corporations

If you are interested in pursuing funding from the private sector, the annual reports of corporations are excellent sources of information. Many large corporations, particularly the Fortune 500 companies, have research offices that conduct studies of interest to the company. If your expertise or area of interest is related to that of the corporation, you might be able to collaborate on one of these studies. In some instances, these offices pursue funding from outside sources; in others they are supported by the company. Annual reports provide information on the amount of money a corporation has devoted to research or educational projects during the past year. They also contain the names and telephone numbers of those to call for more information.

Professional Associations and Other General Sources

Professional Associations and Newsletters

The newsletters of almost all professional associations publish information on upcoming federal or foundation grant programs. They also provide information about their own grant programs. In addition, some associations have an office of research that helps to locate potential funding sources. Others have a governmental affairs office whose staff spends a significant amount of time on Capitol Hill and is knowledgeable about upcoming funding opportunities and current legislative initiatives. These offices are important resources for keeping abreast of changing funding trends.

Professional Meetings

When you attend the annual meeting of your professional organization, talk to funded investigators. They are usually willing to talk about their grantsmanship experiences and to offer advice as to potential funding sources. Associations frequently sponsor workshops on proposal writing at annual meetings that involve participation of representatives of federal agencies. Such forums provide valuable information about current trends and future directions.

Agency Advisory Committees

Many professional associations are able to appoint members of the profession to committees that advise federal agencies. For example, an advisory committee composed of health professionals from a variety of disciplines was convened to help shape the priorities of the recently organized National Center for Medical Rehabilitation Research. If your profession is participating in these activities, they may be tracking the funding priorities and can provide firsthand information about the future directions of many agencies.

The Professional Literature

As a faculty member or practicing health professional, you need to keep current in the professional literature. Knowing the trends in research or education in your profession and area of expertise will help you anticipate new funding directions. These trends often become reflected in the funding environment and therefore help you plan for future calls for proposals.

Electronic Data Bases

Many funding agencies are developing or using electronic data bases to disseminate information about new initiatives or calls for proposals. Private companies have also developed data base programs that allow you to learn about funding sources. Some offer comprehensive services to help faculty members match an area of interest with a funding source. One example is a program called the Sponsored Program Information Network (SPIN). This is a data base of funding opportunities designed to identify external support for research, education, and development projects. It profiles more than 5,000 federal, nonfederal, and corporate funding opportunities. It is designed to match an individual's research interests with funding opportunities through a key word index. SPIN is one of many data bases available to aid in your search for funding. Your university library or office of research information can inform you as to which data base is available.

Newsletters in Specialty Areas

Publications such as *Aging Research and Training News, Educational Bulletin,* or *Chronicle of Higher Education* routinely monitor funding opportunities in a focused area. A subscription to one or more of these sources is helpful.

INTERPRETING CALLS FOR PROPOSALS

Ms. L., in our grant story, has now used a number of these sources to identify potential funding opportunities. While scanning the *Federal Register,* she identifies a call for proposals in the area of her interest. But she is unsure how to interpret the instructions. She has also noticed differences between the federal government and foundations in the specificity of their directions. This is what Ms. L. needs to know about a call for proposals.

Federal Government

To interpret a call for proposals, it is helpful to consider how it is developed by an agency.

The first point to understand is that each federal agency is required to submit an operating budget to Congress that includes plans for the types of programmatic areas the agency hopes to initiate or continue to support. During the budget process, the President and each branch of Congress develops a budget that contains the amount of money that is recommended for authorization to each agency. After a period of budget negotiations, the final authorization is translated into an appropriation. The appropriation is either earmarked for specific programs or left to the discretion of the agency. Funds that are earmarked for a particular programmatic area are then used for the competitions that stimulate a call for proposals.

Generally, a call for proposals is developed by a program officer, who spends considerable time and effort in conducting background work. This background work may involve a thorough review of the literature, a review of findings from previously funded projects related to the topic of the proposed competition, commissioned or invited papers at conferences sponsored by the agency, major government reports such as *Healthy People 2000,* directives contained in major pieces of legislation, or long-range planning meetings sponsored by the agency.

Based on the information obtained, the program officer develops a plan for a competition, which includes a justification of the importance of and need for the project and a description of how the topic fits with the mission of the agency and general interest of the Congress. The plan is then reviewed and revised by others in the agency until there is general approval. The revised plan is then published in the *Federal Register,* and comments from the field are invited. On the basis of these comments, the agency decides how much revision is needed in the initial plan. At this juncture, an agency will know how much money it has to spend and the kind of projects it is interested in funding and will have a general idea about how much money can be targeted to each program area. From this information it is relatively easy to compute the number of projects the agency expects to fund. All of this information will be included in the final call for proposals that will be published.

As a potential applicant, it is important to know that the call for proposals is well thought out and that a program officer has been closely involved in its development. Knowing this makes it incumbent upon any potential applicant to stay current in the literature of his or her field as well as in major government reports and legislation, as these will be the major sources used in the development of a competition. Because the program officer has been so closely involved, he or she will have a very good idea about the kinds of projects that will be successful.

Once you obtain a call for proposals, how do you interpret it? Documents published by the federal government provide information designed to help you write a grant proposal. For example, an announcement of a funding competition in the *Federal Register* contains a description of the objectives of the projects that the agency wants to fund, a list of the types of organizations that are eligible to receive funding, detailed instructions on how to submit a proposal, and the due date of the application. The announcement may also contain information that will help you organize the presentation of your ideas.

If you are submitting a proposal to the Department of Education, the application forms will be found in the *Federal Register.* If you are submitting a research grant to the Public Health Service, you most likely will need to use the standard form, PHS 398. This standard application form can be obtained from the Division of Grants Management, National Institutes of Health, or if you are at a university, from the office of research administration.

Some announcements for competitions indicate that an application kit needs to be requested from the agency. This kit contains the application forms and a program guide that describes the rules and regulations of the competition and the information that must be included in each section of the proposal. These are very important documents and must be read carefully before you begin to write your proposal. You must always follow the suggested outline provided by an agency and organize your application according to the evaluation criteria that are often provided in the application kit. Box 2.1 provides an example of information from an application kit for the Allied Health Projects Grant competition sponsored by the Bureau of Health Professions.

Table 2.3 contains a list of the criteria that the Bureau of Health Professions uses to evaluate proposals submitted in response to the grant program.

TABLE 2.3   Evaluation Criteria

- The extent to which the proposed project meets the legislative purpose
- The background and rationale for the proposed project
- The extent to which the project contains clearly stated realistic and achievable objectives
- The extent to which the project contains a methodology that is integrated and compatible with project objectives, including collaborative arrangements and feasible work plans
- The evaluation plans and procedures for program and trainees if involved
- The administrative and management capability of the applicant to carry out the proposed project, including institutional infrastructure and resources
- The extent to which the budget justification is complete, shows cost-effectiveness and includes cost-sharing when applicable
- Whether there is an institutional plan and commitment for self-sufficiency when federal support ends

BOX 2.1

I. Background and Rationale
    A. Describe the purpose of the project in relation to the legislative purpose (Section 767, PHS Act).
    B. Is a background statement of the national/local need for the proposed project included?
    C. Is the proposed project an appropriate, innovative, effective and efficient means of addressing the problem?
    D. Are the background statement and rationale appropriately researched and referenced in the proposed project?

II. Objectives
    A. What are the objectives?
    B. Are the objectives clearly and concisely stated?
    C. Are the objectives stated in measurable terms and achievable?

III. Project Methods
    A. Are the methods/activities clearly related to the objectives of the proposed project?
    B. Are the methods/activities to accomplish the objectives clearly stated? How will the activities be implemented and accomplished?
    C. Have necessary commitments from cooperating institutions been obtained (e.g., letters of support and memoranda of agreement)?
    D. Are the methods/activities outlined in the proposal the most effective to accomplish the objectives?
    E. Are the methods/activities clearly assigned to the responsible staff? Cooperating institutions?
    F. Is there a feasible time-scheduled work plan included with the proposal?

If you were to submit a proposal to this agency, you would need to become familiar with the legislative purposes of the competition and make sure that your proposal addressed their intent. The proposal should satisfy each of the elements of the evaluation criteria.

Sometimes agencies publish supplemental instructions. These contain changes to program requirements that have been made after an initial program guide has been published. The supplemental instructions may either modify or supplement the requirements in the original set of instructions. The supplement may also contain a more detailed outline of the review criteria that will be used by the review panel, so it is important to pay close attention to such changes.

In some instances, agencies provide advance notice of the competitions they expect to fund in the upcoming year. For example, Table 2.4 summarizes the point values for proposal sections for five different competitions sponsored by the Department of Education (1989), Office of Special Education Programs (OSEP). In the original program announcement, OSEP provided a narrative which described the required proposal sections in each of the five competitions and the point value that would be used in their evaluation.

Table 2.4 demonstrates the point values assigned to each section among the programs. The distribution of points identifies those sections of most importance to the agency. To be competitive, your proposal would have to be particularly strong in the sections with the higher point values. This is not to say that you should ignore those with low point values. For example, to apply to either program 1 or program 4, you would want to expend considerable effort to ensure that your project was technically sound, as this section is worth 35 and 40 points, respectively. If, on the other hand, you developed a proposal for program 5, you would give special attention to describing the importance of your project (worth 20 points) in addition to its technical soundness (worth 30 points). In program 2, three of the sections, Importance,

TABLE 2.4   Proposal Sections and Point Values

Section	Program 1	Program 2	Program 3	Program 4	Program 5
Importance	15	20	10	10	20
Impact	15	05	15	10	10
Technical soundness	35	—	05	40	30
Plan of operation	10	25	25	10	15
Evaluation	05	05	15	05	05
Quality of personnel	10	20	10	10	10
Adequacy of resources	05	10	10	05	05
Budget or cost-effectiveness	05	15	10	10	05

Plan of Operation, and Quality of Personnel, all have relatively high point values (20, 25, and 30 points, respectively).

For some competitions, an agency may request a "letter of intent" to officially inform them of your intention to submit an application. A letter of intent contains a statement that you plan to submit an application and a brief description of the program idea. These letters provide the agency with an indication of how many proposals they may anticipate and will allow better planning as to how to organize the peer review process. It also enables the program officer to provide feedback about your initial ideas. This letter does not commit you to submit a final application, nor will you be evaluated on this idea and told not to submit an application.

Foundations/Professional Associations and Corporations

Each foundation has its own procedure by which it administers programs of funding. Foundations are less constrained by regulations regarding the types of projects they can fund, the way they must process grant applications, and the manner in which they make funding decisions. For many foundations, the instructions for submitting a proposal are much less detailed than those of the federal government. Usually, a foundation asks for a 2–5-page letter describing the project concept. It will then consider this letter carefully and if it is interested will invite you to submit a full proposal.

The lack of detailed instructions does not indicate that foundations have less rigorous expectations about the quality of a grant application than do other agencies. The same care should be taken with proposals to a foundation as with federal grant applications. As in a federal agency, you need to convince the foundation that your project idea is important, that you are the person most qualified to carry it out, and that it fits with the interests of the agency. Prior to submitting a concept paper or letter, it is critical to talk to a foundation program officer about your idea.

Professional associations will vary in the detail and format of their application procedures. If you decide to apply to your association, ask for their application kit or guidelines and read and follow them carefully. The main office of your professional association may also be able to clarify the questions that you may have.

Obtaining corporate support is a different process from gaining federal support. There are more than 160,000 companies that have assets of over $500,000. Each is a highly complex organization with many budgets that could be tapped. Because of this complexity, it is beyond the scope of this book to do more than summarize some suggestions for working with corporations.

Schumacher (1994) cites four distinctions between corporations and federal agencies that make approaches to gaining funding different:

1. Federal granting agencies are required by law to spend a certain amount of money on academic research. Corporations are not, and they are in the business of making money.

2. Federal agencies publicize their external grant program. Most corporations do not even have an external grant program.

3. Federal agencies award a grant to an investigator they have not met. Corporations usually do not fund academic investigators they do not personally know and trust.

4. Only a handful of federal agencies fund individual investigators, whereas there are a vast number of potential sponsors in the private sector.

Obtaining funding from a corporation requires more than a great idea, an excellent research design, a well-written proposal, and an experienced investigator. Although these are important for success, more important is an investigator's ability to form a mutually beneficial and trusting research partnership with a company. Schumacher (1994) claims that the term *partnership* means just what it implies—a truly egalitarian relationship in which trust is established and communication is maintained. As with all approaches to grantsmanship, the development of a partnership takes time; it should start small and build slowly.

Part II

The Perspective of the Grantee

The first step in grantsmanship is to understand the language of the funding environment and the potential sources of funding. The second step is to identify an idea that has the potential for funding. In chapters 3 and 4, we describe the process of grantsmanship from the perspective of the grantee, you and your institution. Chapter 3 describes ways to identify an idea of importance to you and match it to a funding opportunity. Chapter 4 describes the information you need to know about your own institution or agency in order to submit a proposal and administer it should a grant be awarded.

Grantsmanship is viewed as an activity that fosters an individual's personal and professional growth as well as that of his or her discipline, department, institution, or agency. The identification of an idea and the steps necessary to develop this idea into a competitive proposal is presented as part of a broader strategy for personal and professional growth.

Chapter 3

Developing Your Ideas for Funding

One of the most difficult aspects of the process of grantsmanship is identifying an idea that has the potential for funding. There are many ideas that may be interesting, important, or exciting but not necessarily a priority for funding. A great idea is just one ingredient of a competitive proposal. It often must be molded and shaped so that it reflects the priorities of a federal agency, private foundation, or other funding source. However, you should not pursue an idea strictly on the basis of its funding potential. Any idea you develop must fit into your own interests, area of expertise, and plan for professional growth. Therefore, your task is to develop a competitive idea that is consistent with your professional growth plan and corresponds to a funding source.

IDENTIFYING COMPETITIVE IDEAS

Most professionals, whether academic faculty or practitioners, are able to identify topic areas of personal interest. However, identifying an idea that reflects a national and professional need and fitting it to the interests of a funding agency can be more difficult.

Developing an idea with funding potential requires creative and flexible thinking. The following are seven major sources from which to help you formulate a competitive idea:

- Clinical or professional experience
- Professional literature
- Interaction with others
- Societal trends
- Legislative initiatives
- Public documents
- Agency goals and priorities

Clinical or Professional Experience

A very important source of ideas for projects is your own clinical or professional experience. The challenges that emerge in classroom teaching, the persistent issues that arise in working with clients in a clinical setting, or problems identified in staff conferences or faculty meetings often yield important questions. For example, the members of a department of occupational therapy noticed that a persistent topic in their faculty meetings was how differences in knowledge and skills between academic faculty and clinical practitioners often led to misunderstandings between these two groups. They found that faculty in other programs also had identified faculty-practitioner differences as an issue in providing clinical experiences for students. This discovery stimulated members of the department to search for funds to create a training program that would link faculty and clinicians in a way that would minimize these differences and strengthen their relationship.

After reviewing calls for proposals in the *Federal Register* and talking to program officers, two federal agencies were identified that appeared to have an interest in improving the relationship between faculty and practitioners: the Bureau of Health Professions in the Public Health Service and the Office of Special Education and Rehabilitative Services (OSERS) in the Department of Education. One of the six topic areas of interest to the Bureau of Health Professions, Allied Health Special Project Grants, has been to develop innovative models to link allied health clinical practice, education, and research. In response to this interest, faculty in the department of occupational therapy submitted a proposal to develop an interdisciplinary curriculum in geriatrics that involved faculty-clinician teams from four disciplines.

Program officers in the Office of Special Education and Rehabilitation Services also expressed interest in faculty-practitioner cooperation. Another proposal was submitted by the department to develop model clinical sites in which faculty and clinicians would collaborate as a team in training therapists involved in early intervention activities with preschool children.

Professional Literature

Reading the literature in your field is an excellent way to identify pertinent topics. Many professional associations establish both short- and long-term research and education goals for the profession and publish these in their national journals. They also publish policy statements and pertinent articles on current issues. All of these can be used as guides to develop relevant ideas. Regional and national newsletters, such as *OT Week, OT Advance,* and *PT Advance,* are also important sources of information about the current issues in each profession.

For example, *OT Week* periodically publishes a list of research topics that are identified by the American Occupational Therapy Association (AOTA) as important areas for investigation by the profession. These areas have included studies of the effectiveness of practice, cost-effectiveness and reimbursement considerations, program administration, educational improvement, interprofessional relationships, and instrument development. Although these are very broad topics, they identify the general areas of importance to the profession. These broad topics provide a starting point from which to develop specific research questions and projects. One of these areas, practice effectiveness, has also been identified as a funding preference by the American Occupational Therapy Foundation, which is the research arm of AOTA. In this particular case, the professional association not only identified a pertinent issue but also provided grant money to pursue it.

Interaction with Others

Your daily interactions with colleagues might suggest problem areas or issues that could be developed into fundable projects, as the example of the occupational therapy department discussed earlier exemplified. Involvement with individuals from other disciplines is another important source of ideas. Often, these discussions uncover common educational and research issues that are experienced by more than one health profession. Topics that consistently emerge in staff meetings and other discussions often warrant systematic evaluation through a research or education project. In addition to inspiring competitive ideas, professional interactions, especially those that lead to collaborative relationships, may result in programs and proposals that are interdisciplinary in nature. Many federal agencies and foundations are encouraging these collaborative, interdisciplinary approaches in their calls for proposals.

Societal Trends

Societal trends or concerns are also important sources from which to identify a competitive research or educational idea. These trends often signal the possibility that Congress may allocate money to address problems that stimulated these concerns. Consider the current national focus on the high cost of health care and attempts by the Clinton administration to address this problem through health care reform initiatives. The health care reform debate has stimulated many federal agencies to focus on the cost-effectiveness of health care programs, alternative financing mechanisms, and programs of managed care. For example, when health care first emerged as a national issue, the Agency for Health Care Policy and Research (AHCPR) invited applications for research on programs of managed and coordinated care, with an emphasis on costs, quality, and health insurance reform. Many other invitations for research or demonstration programs to test the cost-effectiveness of new health care programs have also been announced, and more will probably be forthcoming. Foundations are also influenced by these societal concerns. For example, the Robert Wood Johnson Foundation has an ongoing interest in health service delivery models for chronic care.

Legislative Initiatives

Because legislative initiatives fuel the funding priorities of federal, state, and local government agencies, it is important to track and examine proposed and pending legislation. For example, the landmark Americans with Disabilities Act (ADA) of 1990 granted critical civil rights to individuals with disabilities. A major component of the act required certain federal agencies to provide technical assistance to organizations to help them understand the ramifications of the ADA. As a result, the Department of Education sponsored a competition that funded a network of 10 ADA technical assistance centers. The Department of Justice also awarded grants for projects aimed at implementing components of the act. As you can see, if your expertise is in any of the areas covered by the ADA, there would be a number of funding opportunities to explore.

Another influential piece of legislation is the Rehabilitation Act of 1973 (PL 93-112), which, in its most recent version, is called the Individuals with Disabilities Education Act (IDEA). Based on the IDEA, the Department of Education sponsors periodic competitions for research studies, in-service seminars, model education programs, and training activities. These competitions involve a range of health professions, including occupational therapy, speech therapy, special education, and physical therapy. Keeping abreast of the amendments and reenactments of this major legislation is important because changes in the act influence funding priorities and spur new areas of investigation.

Public Documents

Public documents and reports by major governmental agencies may also signal impending initiatives. The subjects of the reports and their recommendations can provide major clues to future funding initiatives. Two key documents for health professionals are the Public Health Service report, *Healthy People 2000: National Health Promotion and Disease Prevention Objectives* (published in 1990) and a report from the Institute of Medicine of the National Academy of Sciences called *Allied Health Services: Avoiding Crises.*

Healthy People 2000 was developed over a 3-year period. It contains a "national strategy for significantly improving the health of the nation over the coming decade." This 692-page document, which identifies 22 priority health areas, has influenced the current and planned future funding priorities of many government agencies. Federal agencies under the Public Health Service use this report as a guide and request that proposals address one or more of its priorities. For example, the Bureau of Health Professions, Allied Health Special Project Grants, "Supplement to Instructions to Applicants" included the following statement: "The Public Health Service (PHS) is committed to achieving the health promotion and disease prevention objectives of *Healthy People 2000,* a PHS-led national activity for setting priority areas." Furthermore, applicants to this competition were instructed to describe the relationship of the objectives of their project to the achievement of the objectives outlined in *Healthy People 2000.* This is a clear message that your proposal must address these identified national priorities if it is to be competitive.

The document from the Institute of Medicine, *Allied Health Services: Avoiding Crises,* is another important source of project ideas for health and human service professionals. This report addresses such issues as (a) predicted personnel shortages, (b) the need to attract professionals from underrepresented groups, (c) making health careers more attractive, (d) strengthening education programs, (e) retaining health care workers, and (f) avoiding regulations that impede entry into careers. Each one of these issues could be made the topic of a competitive proposal.

Agency Goals and Priorities

Almost all funding agencies, whether in the private or public sector, set yearly goals and priorities. Many develop long-range plans that specify the types of initiatives they believe are important areas for investigation. These may be published in a variety of ways. Therefore, it is important to contact the funding agency directly to inquire as to whether a document that describes their long-range plans is available for distribution.

WHAT IDEAS ARE HOT AND WHAT ARE NOT

As you examine the seven sources described above, you will begin to see trends from which to identify those ideas that are "hot" or of particular interest to funding agencies. Box 3.1 outlines the areas for which funding is currently available and those ideas or issues that are no longer of significance.

In keeping with the paradigm shift in health care today, funding priorities reflect an emphasis on testing new models of care, those that

BOX 3.1

WHAT IS HOT	WHAT IS NOT
• Community-based service models	• Hospital-based systems
• New health care models (cost-effective patient outcomes)	• Unidiscipline research, service, education approaches
• Underserved populations	• Narrow focus on minorities
• Interdisciplinary team approaches to service, research, education	• Exclusion of women
	• "Doc-top" models
	• Specialty training programs
	• Large overheads
• Innovative health promotion, disease prevention programs	• Operating costs
	• Specialty training programs
• Leveraging funds	• Programs needing continued support
• Self-sufficiency	

are community-based, interdisciplinary, and that examine health promotion and disease prevention strategies. New federal regulations have been implemented that mandate the inclusion of women and minority groups or others who traditionally have been underserved (e.g., rural elderly, urban poor elderly, homeless, American Indians, Pacific Islanders) by the health care system. Funding agencies are also encouraging applications from "teams" of professionals or center grants that involve individuals with different areas of expertise. Also of interest are programs that demonstrate what is called a leveraging of funds, in which existing resources are used to build or expand on a project, and programs that can become self-sufficient after funding is over.

As you begin to identify your area or topic of interest, think of these current funding trends and how you can frame your idea accordingly.

MATCHING IDEAS TO FUNDING PRIORITIES

Let's say you have used one or more of the seven sources we have described to identify an idea for a proposal. You have also conducted a search and found the agencies that are most interested in this area. What do you do now? Matching your idea with a funding interest takes time and creative thinking. It means framing your idea in a way that not only reflects contemporary thought in the field but is also of interest to the agency you have selected. Here are seven steps you might follow to match your idea with the interest of a funding agency (see also Table 3.1).

First, identify a broad topic area through literature searches, discussions with colleagues, and the other sources we have described above. Ask yourself these four questions:

1. Is this idea stimulating and important enough to me so that I would want to spend considerable time thinking and reading?
   If your answer is no, find another idea.

2. Does the idea reflect contemporary thinking in the field?
   If your answer is no, then maybe the idea is interesting but really not that important, or maybe it is one that has been addressed and answered in the literature.

3. Does this idea have long-term potential to be expanded and contribute to my career?
   If you are unsure how to answer this question, consult with a colleague or your supervisor or director.

4. What are the goals of my department, institution, and profession, and how do their goals fit with my topic of interest?
   A response to this question necessitates discussions with representatives of your institution.

Second, based on your responses to the self-study questions above, develop a preliminary list of potential funding agencies. To develop this list, use the *Federal Register, Catalog of Federal Domestic Assistance,* discussions with program officers, the *Foundation Directory,* or electronic data bases.

Third, evaluate your resources by asking yourself these questions:

1. What is my level of expertise, interest, and comfort with this topic area?
   If you need other types of expertise for your program idea, then you may need to develop a team or hire consultants.

2. Are others available to serve as collaborators to complement my level of expertise?
   If your idea is significant to those in your institution, then it

TABLE 3.1   Steps to Match Your Idea with a Funding Agency

1. Identify broad topic areas.
2. Develop preliminary list of potential funding agencies.
3. Evaluate your resources.
4. Narrow your area of interest.
5. Write an abstract.
6. Contact program officers.
7. Reshape your ideas based on conversations and literature review.

should not be difficult to identify others with either complementary expertise or interest.

Fourth, in light of your responses to steps 2 and 3, begin to specify and narrow your area of interest.

Fifth, write an abstract or concept paper that reflects your current thinking. This will help you narrow your topic and force you to describe your idea systematically. This abstract can also be used to obtain feedback from colleagues or program officers.

Sixth, contact program officers from the list of identified competitions that you developed. Discuss your ideas and determine if the idea fits the priorities of the funding agency.

Seventh, begin to reshape your ideas based on these conversations and a further review of the literature.

The following scenario (Box 3.2) describes how this process might be carried out.

BOX 3.2

THE CASE OF MS. S.

Ms. S., who has a master's degree in occupational therapy, is a half-time faculty member. She has an interest in writing a proposal to obtain money to support herself for an additional 50% effort. During the previous year, she secured a $6,000 grant to develop a computer-assisted instructional package in anatomy for occupational therapy students. She also has had experience as a computer consultant on a funded educational program for vocational counselors working with patients with traumatic brain injury (TBI). Ms. S. wants to combine her interests and write a proposal to develop computer-assisted training materials for formal and informal caregivers of patients with TBI. What type of grant should she write and for what agency?

First, Ms. S. has two broad topic areas that interest her: the development of computer-assisted instructional programs and helping formal and informal caregivers of those with TBI. She conducts a data base search for potential funding sources in these two areas and simultaneously begins to assess her level of expertise. She also begins to think about ways to refine these interests.

As a result of her search and assessment process, she makes two discoveries. First, there appears to be greater interest from both federal agencies and foundations in community-based care models for individuals with TBI than in computer-assisted instructional development. That is, most agencies appear more interested in testing model programs than in the development of computer-assisted training materials. Second, she realizes that she does not have sufficient expertise in project development nor substantive background in the area of TBI to submit a research proposal to the agencies she has identified.

Ms. S. knows that if she wants to pursue funding in TBI, she will need to increase her expertise. She decides that her best strategy will be to collaborate with someone with more experience and knowledge. She decides to approach Dr. J., who is the principal investigator of the funded project that involved Ms. S. as the consultant. Ms. S. suggests that her best role in a research study would be as a project manager and offers to take the lead in developing the ideas and the grant application. Ms. S. also wants to examine the potential of using her expert knowledge in computer-assisted technology in this research project. Dr. J. is very receptive to this idea because it has the potential to extend her current grant and is compatible with her personal research goals.

Ms. S. and Dr. J. meet and discuss several possible ideas. Ms. S. reviews relevant literature and then writes a one-page abstract, which she shares with other colleagues to obtain feedback. She then telephones the program officers of the federal agencies and foundations she had identified earlier. Based on these discussions, she refines her idea for a project and begins to develop her proposal in more detail.

PROFESSIONAL GROWTH STRATEGIES

Developing your ideas for funding should be part of a long-range plan for professional growth and development. Writing a grant proposal represents a significant investment of your time and effort. It should, therefore, be an activity that enhances your career and professional goals. It is important to remember that developing skill in writing a grant proposal is compatible with the goals of a health and human service professional.

In identifying an idea for a grant proposal, think about what you want to accomplish in 2, 3, or 5 years. One grant proposal, especially if it is funded, should serve as a building block for another. Each grant should be part of a larger plan that provides incremental personal and professional growth and experience. Table 3.2 outlines four components of a strategy for professional growth.

Develop a Plan for Long-Range Personal Development. To develop a plan for professional growth, begin with an outline of your career or professional goals. Ask yourself the following questions: (1) What do I want to be doing 3 to 5 years from now? (2) Am I more interested in research, teaching, or clinical work? Although research, teaching, and clinical work are interrelated, you may want to place more emphasis in one of these areas. The area you select will then influence the type of grant you choose to develop.

As you identify your career goals and develop your plan, talk to your supervisor, department head, and/or director. Engage in a dialogue in which they clarify for you their own expectations and goals, and those of the department and the institution as a whole. From these discussions, you will have a better idea of how compatible your goals

TABLE 3.2   Components of a Professional Growth Strategy

1. Develop a plan for long-range personal development and your role as a faculty member. What do you want to be doing 3 to 5 years from now?

2. Build individual credentials:
   - Allow time and patience.
   - Present papers at professional meetings.
   - Develop presentations into publications.
   - Write a book review or column for your professional newsletter.
   - Serve as a reviewer of abstracts that are submitted to a professional meeting.
   - Serve as a reviewer for a grant competition (start with competitions that are sponsored by your professional association).

3. Build a track record of funding:
   - Start by competing for small intramural grant awards.
   - Try to obtain small extramural grant awards.

4. Work on teams with more experienced researchers.

are with those of your department or institution, and you will get a sense of the amount of institutional support you are likely to receive as you pursue grant funding. These discussions will also help you decide on the types of grants to explore. For example, if you are interested in curriculum development and your department values and supports educational innovation, then you will probably receive the institutional support necessary to pursue a training grant. If, on the other hand, your department has a greater interest in research, you will need to rethink your goals and perhaps develop your research skills or examine your curriculum interests from a research perspective.

Build Individual Credentials. Building your credentials requires time and patience. When you submit a grant, the peer review panel will look closely at your credentials as part of the evaluation process. For example, Box 3.3 contains a typical comment by a review panel regarding the credentials of an investigator who did not demonstrate sufficient expertise in the topic of his proposal, congestive heart failure and a nursing home-based intervention.

Building your credentials in a field can be done by (1) presenting papers at professional meetings, (2) developing these presentations for publication, (3) writing a book review or column for your professional newsletter, (4) serving as a reviewer of abstracts for a professional meeting, and (5) serving as a reviewer for a grant competition.

Build a Track Record of Funding. Part of building your personal credentials involves developing a funding track record.

BOX 3.3

> The principal investigator, Dr. T., has a PhD in sociology and is an assistant professor. His past experience has included extensive research in gerontology and health care interventions for stroke patients. However, he has no previous research experience or publications on nursing, home care, or congestive heart failure. There is no doctorally prepared nurse on the project, which is also a problem. In particular, the team lacks clinical research expertise with congestive heart failure patients. The project would be enhanced by collaboration with someone from the college of nursing.

Once you have found an idea and an agency, you also need to show the agency that you are capable of successfully implementing the idea. Funding agencies require that an applicant demonstrate that he or she has the expertise to carry out the proposed project. Therefore, they will look for what is called a "track record," or prior successful experience, in the content area for which funds are requested. This track record is usually evaluated by the number of professional presentations and publications you have in the area or by previous funding experience.

It can be difficult to obtain funding unless you have been funded in the past. Fortunately, there are ways to break this "Catch 22" cycle. First, start small. Find out what funding opportunities are available through your own institution. Many hospitals and colleges give "seed money" to beginning investigators to conduct pilot projects. This money is provided through what are called intramural competitions. Usually, these competitions are for small amounts of money. However, even $200 can go a long way to support a mail survey or needs assessment.

Also, find out what funding opportunities exist from your professional association. Many professional associations have money to support projects in areas of importance to the profession. Do not hesitate to call your association to inquire about these programs and the possibility of obtaining technical assistance from staff members.

In addition to helping you establish a funding track record, these small grants provide two other important advantages. First, they provide you with experience in conducting a funded project. Second, they can supply pilot data that can be used to justify the need for more funds to continue or expand your project. The inclusion of pilot data in a proposal demonstrates that you have mastered the content area and that you have tested or evaluated components of your idea. It also substantiates the need for a larger project to advance an important area of inquiry.

Work on Teams with More Experienced Researchers.   Another important strategy to enhance your credentials and improve your grant-writing skills is to work with others who have more experience than you. If you find an investigator who is planning to submit a proposal, volunteer your services, as did Ms. S. in the earlier example. Offer to do anything on the team that will make a contribution. You will find that most experienced investigators will welcome your help if you have something to offer. Becoming a member of an investigative team will also give you a track record in grant work and allow you to obtain important insight regarding how proposals are written. If the proposal is funded, you will also gain invaluable experience in the administration of a funded program. Take the time to learn from these more knowledgeable investigators.

Chapter 4

Learning about Your Institution

As we discussed in chapter 2, funding agencies have detailed instructions, requiring careful attention, that guide the submission of proposals. However, your agency or institution also has rules about submitting a proposal. These rules involve who in the institution is required to approve your grant submission, what needs to be requested in a budget, and what procedures must be followed for the protection of human subjects involved in the project.

Your institution also has policies to be followed should your project be funded. They involve procedures about recruiting and hiring personnel, reporting grant-related expenses, and submitting required budget reports. Therefore, knowing the policies and procedures of your institution early in the proposal development process will help you work productively at both the preaward and postaward stages.

QUESTIONS TO ASK OF YOUR INSTITUTION

Table 4.1 lists the most important questions to ask your supervisor, department head, or other administrators to learn about the rules of your institution or agency.

TABLE 4.1   Seven Questions to Ask About Your Institution

1. What are the procedures you must follow to obtain approval for a grant application from an official in the institution?
2. Who in the institution has to review and approve your budget? What resources are available to help you prepare a budget?
3. If your application requires hiring new personnel, what procedures must you follow?
4. Once a grant is received, how are the funds administered? Which office monitors the budget and prepares the final budget reports that are required by the funding agency?
5. What are the institution's procedures for processing payment of grant expenses?
6. What are the policies regarding the distribution of indirect cost?
7. What other policies related to the implementation of grants are there?

Let's examine each of these questions.

1. *What are the procedures you must follow to obtain approval for a grant application from an official in the institution?* A grant is never awarded to an individual but to that person's institution. It is the institution that must assume legal responsibility for the conduct of the project and the expenditure of funds. Therefore, every application that is submitted must be signed by an official who is the legal representative of the institution. Prior to the submission of a grant, you will need to determine who in your institution must sign the face sheet of the application. Many universities have an "office of research administration" that reviews all applications prior to their submission. Other institutions require that a draft of the grant be provided to the signing official a week or more in advance of its due date. Still others may require a meeting to discuss the grant prior to obtaining the official signature.

2. *Who in the institution has to review and approve your budget? What resources are available to help you prepare a budget?* Developing a budget can be complex, especially if you are hiring consultants or entering into agreements with other institutions. In some institutions, the office of research administration or office of budget administration will provide technical assistance or actually develop a budget for a grant application. Even if someone else in your institution assumes responsibility for creating your budget, you should obtain the following information:

- Fringe benefit rate of your institution
- Allowable percentage of increase for yearly salaries
- Salary figures for personnel on the grant
- Indirect recovery cost rate of your institution
- Travel reimbursement rate granted by your institution

We discuss budget preparation and these issues in more detail in chapter 6.

3. *If your application requires hiring new personnel, what procedures must you follow?* Although you do not need this information in order to submit the application, it is still best to learn about procedures prior to a grant submission. The human resource or personnel department usually has stringent rules and regulations for hiring new personnel. This department can also show you how to write a job description that fits your requirements and how to advertise for the position if necessary, as well as indicating the salary range that would be appropriate and approved by the institution.

4. *Once a grant is received, how are the funds administered? Which office monitors the budget and prepares the final budget reports that are required by the funding agency?* When you receive a grant award, your institution will usually maintain the official budget, disburse your funds, make the appropriate financial reports, and monitor your expenditures. However, you still need to maintain a working budget, so you should inquire about the kind of reporting you can expect. For example, some institutions keep track of all expenditures and provide the investigator with weekly, biweekly, or monthly reports. Other institutions expect the department and/or individual investigator to establish an accounting mechanism, although all payments still have to be approved by the financial officer. The procedures that are followed in your institution will shape what you will need to do to control your budget.

5. *What are the institution's procedures for processing payment of grant expenses?* This information is important for meeting your financial obligations, such as payment to other institutions or consultants or for ordering equipment and other supplies in a timely manner. Each institution has its own forms, time lines, set of procedures, and requirements for official signatures. Knowing

these procedures will help establish a financial structure from which to administer your grant and will expedite many administrative details.

6. *What are the policies regarding the distribution of indirect cost?* In some institutions, the individual or the department that receives the grant is given a percentage of the indirect costs to assist in administering the grant application. For example, let's say the department of occupational therapy in a university received a grant award for which the university will obtain a 60% cost recovery rate. In some cases, 10% of this rate is given back to the department to help offset the additional but hidden costs associated with grant administration. In other instances, it is given back to the investigator to use as discretionary money. However, this policy differs among institutions, and in many cases, indirect costs are not shared with the investigator or department.

7. *What other policies exist that are related to the implementation of grants?* As you plan your first grant submission, set up a series of information-gathering meetings with key administrators or individuals in your agency who may be involved in either the preaward or implementation phase of your grant. For example, the reference librarian will be an invaluable guide to available information services. Also, meet with individuals in the budget department, sponsored programs, the office of research administration, the office of the dean, and human resource department to discuss your grant program and how it might affect their departments. In addition to furnishing you with information about various administrative procedures, these individuals may be able to provide valuable suggestions that will save you time and effort if your proposal is funded.

INSTITUTIONAL REVIEW BOARD PROCEDURES

If you are developing a research proposal involving human subjects, you will need to submit a protocol to your institutional review board (IRB) for its approval. In some institutions, the IRB may be called the human subjects board or the research committee. According to federal regulation, all research involving human subjects that is funded by the government must be approved by an IRB or comparable committee. Most institutions extend this regulation to include any research, whether funded by an outside source or conducted independently of funding. Therefore, prior to conducting your research, IRB approval must be obtained. An IRB is composed of individuals with diverse areas of expertise in biomedical and behavioral research who review each research protocol developed at the institution. The purpose of an IRB review is to ensure that the rights and welfare of the subjects in a study are protected and that the benefits of the research are greater than any risk associated with participation. The IRB evaluates each aspect of a research protocol, including the consent form, advertisements for subject recruitment, data collection procedures, and aspects of the study design. The IRB also conducts an annual review of the progress of each approved research protocol to evaluate such things as the number of subjects recruited, the incidence of adverse reactions, and the identification of new risks. Although stringent, this review is particularly critical in drug studies and the testing of new medical procedures; it is also very important to behavioral and social science studies in which human beings are involved.

Prior to submitting a research application to a funding agency, you should learn about the internal procedures that have been established by your institution for reviewing and approving research projects. If you plan to study subjects from other clinical sites, you must also discover the IRB requirements of each of these sites. Although many clinical sites do not have a formal IRB, they will usually have some form of human subjects board, such as a committee that reviews and approves requests for conducting research on its premises.

It is also important to read the directions of an application carefully to determine if IRB approval is required prior to the grant submission. Some competitions will require that IRB approval be obtained *prior* to the submission of the application, whereas others will stipulate that submission to and approval by the IRB occur within 30 days of the grant submission. Even if IRB approval is not required prior to the grant submission, it is prudent to complete the IRB requirements as you are developing your grant application, because similar information is required for both the IRB and the funding agency.

Although each institution establishes its own set of procedures for the submission and review of research protocols, there are three different levels of an IRB review. The type of review—full, expedited, or exempt—you receive will depend on the degree of risk associated with the research procedures. Each review will differ in the number and type of individuals who must read and approve the research protocol. A *full review* involves a review by all members of the IRB (perhaps up to 20 individuals). Usually, one member is assigned as primary reviewer and one or more members are assigned as secondary reviewers. The primary reviewer presents the protocol to the entire board with input from the secondary reviewers as to its strength and weakness. A full review is required if the research protocol involves one or more of the following groups or categories: (a) infants/fetuses, (b) children, (c) pregnant women, (d) prisoners, (e) mentally incompetent individuals, (f) addicted persons, (g) HIV testing and AIDS, and (h) research involving investigational drugs or medical devices.

An *expedited review* is carried out by a subcommittee appointed from the full board. Studies that qualify for an expedited review are those that involve only minimal risks to subjects, such as (a) recording data from individuals 18 years or older using noninvasive procedures that are routinely used in clinical practice; (b) the study of existing data, documents, and specimens; (c) individual or group behavior or characteristics of individuals where the investigator does not manipulate subjects' behavior and the research does not involve stress to the subject.

Research protocols that are determined by the IRB as *exempt* are usually reviewed by the chairperson or another appointed member of the IRB. These studies are not monitored on a regular basis as long as the investigator continues to follow the protocol that was originally proposed, although informing the IRB of such studies is mandatory. Categories of research that are considered exempt from full or expedited review include research involving the following activities: (a) normal educational practices, (b) survey or interview procedures, (c) observation of public behavior, and (d) collection or study of existing data.

Each institution establishes its own set of procedures for submitting research protocols to its IRB. Some require that the entire grant application be submitted to the IRB for review and that the principal investigator meet with the board to present the study and respond to questions. Other IRBs require that an abstract, informed consent, and a response to six basic questions be submitted for review. The basic information that most IRBs need in order to adequately review a study protocol is outlined in Box 4.1.

Let's examine the six questions in Box 4.1. These also must be answered in Section 8 (Human Subjects) of the PHS 398 form, which is used for research grant submissions to the National Institutes of Health, and in human subject sections of grant applications for other

BOX 4.1

BASIC COMPONENTS OF AN IRB SUBMISSION
COVER SHEET:

Title of project, funding source, names of investigators, estimated budget and budget period, indication of use of human or animal subjects or FDA-approved devices or drugs, and the signature of key officials (investigators, department chairs, etc.).

ABSTRACT:
Summary of the research, its significance and purpose, specific questions and hypotheses, recruitment procedures, subject inclusion criteria, statistical analyses.

INFORMED CONSENT:
Consent form for use with all subjects in the study. A consent form outlines the study procedures in lay language and informs subjects of their right to withdraw from the study protocol and the risks and benefits to participation.

RESPONSE TO SIX QUESTIONS:
1. *What is the proposed involvement of human subjects and their characteristics?*
2. *What are the sources of research material obtained from individually identifiable living human subjects in the form of specimens, records, or data?*
3. *What are the plans for recruitment of subjects?*
4. *What are the potential risks—physical, psychological, social, legal, or other?*
5. *What are the procedures for protecting against or minimizing any potential risks?*
6. *Why are the risks to subjects reasonable in relation to the anticipated benefits to subjects?*

agencies. These questions require the investigator to specify the procedures of the study as they relate to the recruitment of human subjects, data collection, issues of confidentiality, and the risk/benefit ratio of study participation.

1. *What is the proposed involvement of human subjects and their characteristics?* The investigator is asked to describe the study population and to list and justify specific inclusion and exclusion

criteria. If your study involves a special population, you must justify why this particular population is required. If your study excludes certain individuals, such as women or minority populations, you must justify their exclusion. Also, you are asked to discuss the basic characteristics of the subjects you plan to recruit.

2. *What are the sources of research material obtained from individually identifiable living human subjects in the form of specimens, records, or data?* This question requires the investigator to identify the type of data that will be collected and the procedures that will be followed for obtaining information. Box 4.2 provides an example of a response to this question.

3. *What are the plans for recruitment of subjects?* Here the investigator is asked to specify the plan for recruiting subjects. If advertisements are used, the IRB must approve the wording of all recruitment pieces to assure that it is not misleading or coercive in nature. Also, if compensation is provided to subjects, a clear explanation of the procedures, including how much and when subjects will be compensated, should be given. Box 4.3 provides an example of a response to this question.

4. *What are the potential risks—physical, psychological, social, legal, or other?* The investigator must indicate all known and potential risks associated with participation in the study. In studies for which there is significant risk, detailed information must be provided regarding the nature and extent of each risk and the statistical probability of its occurrence. Detailed documentation from studies that have demonstrated these risks

BOX 4.2

EXAMPLE OF DISCUSSION OF SOURCES OF RESEARCH MATERIAL

The primary source of research material involves two 2-hour personal interviews that will be conducted in the subject's home by a trained member of the research team at Time 1 (baseline) and Time 2 (4 months from baseline). The interview protocol will involve a series of structured and standardized scales reflecting domains such as functional level, depression, and health.

BOX 4.3

EXAMPLE OF DESCRIPTION OF A RECRUITMENT PLAN

Subjects will be recruited by using a set of procedures developed by the investigators that have been used successfully to obtain subjects for other large-scale studies. These procedures involve the systematic outreach to an array of social services, medical centers, senior centers, and regional media sources to recruit eligible participants by using advertisements and letters inviting participation. Interested individuals will be instructed to contact the project manager by telephone. Eligibility will be determined by a brief (20-minute) telephone screen administered to individuals who call and express interest in study participation. This screen will determine level of functioning and difficulties experienced in carrying out daily activities, falls history, and mental status. For those individuals who are eligible to participate, an explanation of the purpose of the study, the time commitment, financial remuneration, randomization procedures, and nature of participation in the experimental and minimal treatment conditions will be given. Informed consent will be obtained in person at the time of the first interview.

must be carefully described as well. Box 4.4 provides an example of a discussion of a low-risk study.

BOX 4.4

EXAMPLE OF DISCUSSION OF MINIMAL RISK

There are no known risks associated with participation in this study. There are no physical, psychological, social, or legal risks associated with the structured interviews. Occasionally, the content of the questions may raise personal and emotional issues for an older adult. Such responses to interview content, however, have not been found to pose a serious psychological threat. Interviewers are carefully trained to handle such issues sensitively and to facilitate the participant's ability to complete the interview successfully.

5. *What are the procedures for protecting against or minimizing any potential risks?* An investigator must not only identify all potential risks associated with study participation but must also develop a set of procedures to protect against or minimize the potential occurrence of each risk that is posed. As part of this discussion, the investigator should describe procedures for maintaining subject confidentiality, as shown in Box 4.5.

6. *Why are the risks to subjects reasonable in relation to the anticipated benefits to subjects?* Finally, in this last question, the investigator is requested to explain why the anticipated benefits of the study outweigh the potential risks associated with participation. The investigator may explain the immediate benefits to subject participation (e.g., financial compensation, opportunity to participate in meaningful experience, opportunity to receive a new treatment), as well as the long-term expected outcomes (e.g., discovery of new drug or treatment that would benefit a clinical population or make a significant contribution to the body of knowledge regarding a disease).

Most studies involving human subjects will also require the use of an informed-consent form. A consent form is a legal docu-

BOX 4.5

EXAMPLE OF DISCUSSION OF PROTECTION OF CONFIDENTIALITY

Precoded data collection instruments will be prepared for use with subjects at each testing occasion. Identification numbers to assure subject confidentiality will be used. Only one master log—containing the subject name, address and telephone number, and study identification assignment—will be maintained. This log, in both hard copy and disk, will be stored in a locked filing cabinet separate from other identifying information. All completed data collection instruments will be stored in filing cabinets as well and kept locked in the Center for Collaborative Research. Audiotaping of intervention sessions will be identified by numbers only, and any transcriptions resulting from these tapes will not contain any references to names or other personal identifying information.

---

ment that informs a subject about the study procedures and its risks and benefits. By signing this form, subjects acknowledge that they understand that they have volunteered for participation and can refuse to participate or withdraw from the study at any time. Before you develop your own consent form, consult with your IRB to inquire whether a particular format is required. Box 4.6 outlines the 13 basic elements that are included in any type of informed consent.

BOX 4.6

ELEMENTS OF INFORMED CONSENT

1. Name of project.
2. Introduction and purpose of study.
3. Procedures/treatments.
4. Time commitment.
5. Right of refusal.
6. Risks/discomforts associated with study participation.
7. Description of benefits to subjects.
8. Explanation of compensation for participation (if relevant).
9. Statement regarding protection of subject confidentiality.
10. Final statement that subject has read and understood the form and has received a copy.
11. Names and telephone numbers of investigators or of a person to contact if there are questions.
12. Signature of subject and date.
13. Signature of witness and date.

1. *Name of project.* The name of the study project should be written so that it can be understood by a lay person. Some investigators state the scientific title of the project first and then provide its translation into lay language.

2. *Study purpose.* The purpose of the study should be clearly stated so that it is easily understood by a lay person.

3. *Procedures.* Each procedure must be accurately described so that subjects understand the full extent of their participation.

4. *Time.* The time involved in each procedure as well as the total length of time for the study should be described.

5. *Refusal.* Subjects must be informed that they have the right to refuse to participate in the study and that refusal will not affect their right to medical treatment or any other type of service. Also, subjects must be informed of their right to withdraw from participation at any time without penalty, as well as their right to refuse to respond to interview questions.

6. *Risks/discomforts.* Subjects are informed about any risks associated with participation as well as any discomforts that may be experienced. Each risk should be carefully explained, along with a description of alternative treatments that may be available.

7. *Benefits.* An informed consent describes any immediate or long-term benefits to subjects. Benefits may include participation in a particular treatment, contribution to the research process, or other, more tangible benefits.

8. *Explanation of compensation.* The compensation for study participation, if relevant, must be clearly specified so that subjects understand the circumstances under which they can expect remuneration.

9. *Subject confidentiality.* The investigator must discuss the procedures that will be used to assure confidentiality of the information that is collected. For example, the use of identification numbers to refer to subjects and keeping all subject data in locked filing cabinets are two important and traditional research procedures that should be discussed in a consent form.

Part III

Writing the Proposal

The next four chapters contain the *heart of the matter:* writing the proposal. Each chapter covers a different aspect of writing, including an in-depth discussion of the basic sections of an application (chapter 5), a description of the elements of a budget (chapter 6), technical considerations and administrative matters (chapter 7), and strategies for writing effectively and concisely (chapter 8).

Writing and presenting your ideas in a concise, clear manner is one of the most important components of the process of grantsmanship. Proposal writing involves a style that is technical, crisp, and to the point. It is not an occasion to use a more literary, flowery, or embellished approach to writing. The importance of writing is highlighted by a study conducted by the Bureau of Health Professions (Brand, Clark, Paavola, & Pitts, 1992) that examined the strengths and weaknesses raised by review panels of proposals submitted to the Allied Health Special Project Grants competition. Six major weaknesses were noted by reviewers in the allied health grants:

Weaknesses	*Percentage of applications*
Background and rationale are poorly referenced.	26.4
Objectives are not clear or are confusing.	22.9
Project methods are not well detailed or developed.	39.4
Evaluation is vague: specific criteria not identified.	22.3
Plan for self-sufficiency is not included.	50.0
Commitment of other agencies is not identified.	40.5

Including a plan for self-sufficiency is a technical requirement of proposals submitted to this particular agency. However, the other five weaknesses are those commonly found in all proposals and are particularly revealing. As you can see, the weaknesses concern the *quality* of writing and the presentation of the content of the applicant's ideas. Unclear or confusing objectives, undeveloped methods, poorly referenced background and rationale, and vague evaluation criteria are all weaknesses that can be improved by attention to the process of writing a proposal.

Chapter 5

Common Sections of Proposals

O nce you have identified a competitive idea for a research, education, or demonstration project, it is time to write the proposal. As with other aspects of grantsmanship, writing a competitive proposal is a systematic process. A proposal is simply a document in which you "propose" to carry out an idea. The proposal should present a compelling case that will persuade a funding agency to support your idea.

Agencies are interested in funding the best ideas from among those that are submitted. To help identify the best ideas, the agencies provide the information that should be included in a proposal. This information and the format in which it is presented help reviewers make judgments regarding the importance and quality of your idea and to compare one proposal with all the others that are submitted. Although each agency develops its own format, there are sections that are common to most proposals.

DESCRIPTION OF SECTIONS

The sections of a proposal can be thought of as a series of questions that you answer.

- What is your project about?
- Why is it important?
- What will you do?
- How will you do it?
- What will it cost?
- Why will it cost what it does?
- Why are you the best one to do it?

The instructions for a grant proposal are a series of directions to help you answer these questions. Keeping these questions in mind and following the directions of the agency as you write will help you focus on the important points to make.

As discussed in chapter 2, a federal agency informs applicants about how a proposal should be organized through its call for proposals. Some agencies, particularly in the Public Health Service, publish a program guide that contains detailed information about what is expected in the proposal. Agencies will occasionally issue supplemental instructions to this guide if there are changes in their requirements after the program guide goes to press or if a specific competition has additional requirements. Always check to see if there are supplemental instructions. Other agencies, such as those in the Department of Education, publish an application in the *Federal Register* and include specific instructions for its completion in the announcement. To submit to a foundation, request their application kit. The instructions for almost all competitions provide a comprehensive description of the proposal sections that are required, and they usually specify the page length of each section and/or the maximum number of pages of the entire proposal.

It is critical that the published guidelines from an agency be followed closely. In some competitions, you can lose points or, in the worst case, be disqualified from the competition if you have not conformed to the agency's specifications. Therefore, prior to writing the proposal, read all the instructions carefully and be sure that you understand them. If you are unclear about what is required as part of the grant submission, call the project officer to clarify vague points.

A call for proposals or application kit often includes the rating system that will be used by the members of a review panel to evaluate your proposal. Some agencies may assign point values to each section. As discussed in chapter 2, the evaluative points indicate the relative importance of each section.

Although there is great variation among proposal formats, the sections that are commonly found in federal grant applications are listed in Box 5.1. Each of these sections answers one or more of the questions we posed earlier:

BOX 5.1

Title
Abstract
Introduction
Goals/Objectives/Specific Aims
Background/Significance/Importance
Literature Review/Theoretical Foundation
Methodology/Research or Educational Plan
Dissemination Plan
Plan of Management
Investigative Team Credentials
Institutional Qualifications
Budget
References
Appendix Material

Let's examine each of these sections.

Title

The title of a proposed project may sound like a simple thing to write. However, it can be difficult to capture the main idea of the proposal in a short phrase. The title describes the main idea of your project so that it orients the reviewer as to what he or she is about to read. It should not be so brief that it says nothing, nor so long that a reviewer has to work hard to figure out what it means. Box 5.2 shows examples of three titles.

Some agencies have specific requirements about the length of the title. For example, grants submitted to the National Institutes of Health (NIH) that use the PHS 398 form stipulate a title that is descriptive and specific rather than general. On this form, the title is not

BOX 5.2

Too brief:
"A Program to Help Individuals Who Are Homeless"

Too long and convoluted:
"A Program to Understand the Health Care Needs of Those Who are Homeless by Working with Four Homeless Shelters and Developing Educational Materials for Students in Dental Hygiene, Nursing, Occupational Therapy, and Physical Therapy Programs"

Just right:
"A Community and Academic Partnership: A Program to Train Interdisciplinary Health Care Teams to Provide Services to Individuals Who Are Homeless"

---

allowed to exceed 56 typewritten spaces, including punctuation and spaces between words.

Abstract

The abstract is a brief description of the proposal. Generally, the abstract contains a statement of the purpose of your study or project and a brief description of the research design or methods that will be used to carry it out. Although each agency may differ in its requirement, there is usually a limit on the number of words that can be used (approximately 500). Therefore, the abstract must be very clear and succinct.

The abstract is very important because it is the first section of a proposal that a reviewer will read, and it often leaves a lasting impression. An abstract that is not clearly written or is filled with mistakes or typographical errors gives the reviewer a poor impression that may influence how the rest of the proposal is evaluated. Because the abstract represents an executive summary of the entire project, it should be the last section you write. Box 5.3 is an example of an abstract.

BOX 5.3

EXAMPLE OF AN ABSTRACT

The purpose of this project is to develop, implement, and evaluate a new program by which to educate physical therapy, occupational therapy, dental hygiene, and nursing students in interdisciplinary, community-based health care for homeless individuals. The program is based on a five-stage collaborative model that links allied health and nursing faculty, community organizations serving the homeless, and social workers in homeless shelters. The purpose of this partnership is to develop and implement innovative curricular activities for nursing and allied health students on interdisciplinary approaches to community health, including health promotion and restoration services. This 3-year program will be carried out in three phases: a developmental phase in which a partnership will be formed among faculty and community participants, an implementation phase in which a curricular program in interdisciplinary community-based health care generated in the first phase is implemented, and an evaluation phase in which the program is evaluated, the results disseminated to the academic and clinical communities, and the education model applied to other underserved populations.

Introduction

Most proposals begin with an introductory paragraph that provides the reader with a general overview of the main idea of the project and its importance. In this section you address the questions of what your project is about and why it is important. For example, as the abstract in Box 5.3 suggests, let's say you propose to develop a project that brings together university faculty and social workers in homeless shelters to plan a curriculum to provide education for students in nursing and allied health who are interested in working in these shelters. An opening introductory paragraph might discuss the increasing number of persons who are homeless in the United States and in the city in

which the project will be held, the lack of health and social service personnel who are adequately prepared to work with this population, and the limited content in the curriculum of disciplines such as occupational therapy, physical therapy, nursing, and dental hygiene. Although this section is brief, it is appropriate to cite data from sources such as national studies or reports and statements from professional groups.

Goals/Objectives/Specific Aims

If you are applying for training money, this section contains the goals and objectives of the educational program. There is often confusion as to the difference between a goal, an objective, and an activity.

A training or educational program must be based on one or more goals. A *goal* is a statement that reflects what will be accomplished as a result of the program. It is a global, or broad, statement describing what will be accomplished. In turn, each goal has a specific set of objectives. An *objective* is a statement about an outcome of the program that can be evaluated or measured. That is, an objective must be measurable and therefore should be written in such a way as to show that it can be evaluated. An objective usually includes words such as "increase," "describe," "enable," "enhance." Each objective is accomplished by conducting a number of *activities*. These activities should lead to the objectives, which in turn should lead to and define the goal. Therefore, if the activities are accomplished and objectives achieved, the goal of the program will have been attained. An example of a goal, two of its objectives, and representative activities are shown in Box 5.4.

If you propose to conduct a research study, present specific aims. Aims are similar to goals in that they describe concisely and realistically what will be accomplished in your research project. In addition to specifying the aims of the study, you will also need to state specific hypotheses that will be tested. These hypotheses, when tested, should provide answers to the questions inherent in the aims of your study and show that you have accomplished what you set out to do. An example of a specific aim and an accompanying hypothesis are shown in Box 5.5.

If you propose to conduct a study using a qualitative methodology in which formal hypothesis testing is not appropriate, you will need to explain this point carefully to reviewers. Although there is a developing awareness among review panels of the scientific value of quali-

BOX 5.4

Goal: The goal of this project is to prepare future occupational therapists, nurses, physical therapists, and dental hygienists to collaborate in delivering health promotion and health restoration services to persons who are homeless in community shelters.

Objective 1: To increase students' knowledge base of biological, psychological, cultural, and social influences on providing adequate health services to persons who are homeless.
Activity: This objective will be accomplished through the following activities:

1. Student participation in specific departmental courses that provide the necessary professional knowledge, skills, and attitudes for working with the diverse population of individuals who are homeless.
2. Student participation in three core multidisciplinary courses that relate theory, health policy, and research in the delivery of community-based health services.

Objective 2: To enable students to collaborate effectively as members of an interdisciplinary health care team.
Activity: This objective will be accomplished through student participation in two team-building courses designed to move students from a unidisciplinary to an interdisciplinary perspective.

tative research, the formats for most proposals favor a quantitative or linear structure for the research process.

If you are submitting an application to the NIH, the specific aims section must not exceed one single-spaced typed page. This makes it even more imperative that you be very concise.

Goals, objectives, and/or aims are critical building blocks of a proposal. They provide the review panel with a clear picture of what you plan to accomplish in the project. After you have written this section, ask yourself the questions presented in Box 5.6 as a way of reflecting on your work and of making sure that you have presented sound goals, objectives, and/or aims.

BOX 5.5

Specific aim: To test the immediate and long-term effects of a home-based occupational therapy intervention for 250 caregivers of elderly dementia patients, using a randomized experimental two-group design.

Hypothesis: Caregivers of elderly dementia patients participating in a home-based intervention program will exhibit significantly less stress than will caregivers of elderly dementia patients who receive telephone instructions.

BOX 5.6

SELF-STUDY QUESTIONS

1. Are the goals, objectives, and/or aims clearly defined?
2. Are the key concepts/constructs defined?
3. Do the objectives, when taken together, define the goal of the study?
4. Will the hypotheses, when tested, accomplish the aims of the study?
5. Are the independent/dependent variables operationally defined?
6. Is the terminology used for the operational definitions clear and unambiguous?
7. Are the hypotheses/objectives stated in observable, measurable terms?
8. Are the hypotheses based on a sound theoretical framework?
9. Do the hypotheses clearly predict a relationship between variables?

Rationale/Significance/Importance

There is usually a section in a grant application that requires a demonstration of the importance of the idea or its significance. Having an idea that is exciting to you is a necessary starting point in writing the proposal, but this idea also must be considered important to the funding agency. If a separate section is not specified, it is still in your best interest to find a way to tell the review panel why your project is important. If a section on significance is not required, a good place to put this discussion is in your introduction. After you introduce your idea, develop a logical, clear, and compelling argument for the necessity of your project. Make this argument so persuasive that reviewers will not ask the "so what" question. The "so what" question concerning the significance and importance of a project represents a fatal flaw. If a reviewer cannot answer the "so what" question by reading your rationale, your project has a poor chance of being funded.

In a training or education project, the significance of an idea is usually established by citing important research reports, professional literature, local and national data, and other government statistics that demonstrate a need for the project idea. If there is little data available, you may need to conduct a survey or needs assessment to document this significance (see chapter 7). Even a small-scale or local survey helps to substantiate the need for and value of your program.

The significance of a research idea is justified through a concise review of studies that highlight the level of knowledge of the field and the need for further research. These studies should demonstrate that your question is important and one that has not been satisfactorily answered. If you have conducted any small-scale or pilot studies on the topic, including the results as part of your argument would make your proposal more competitive (see chapter 7).

Literature Review/Theoretical Foundation

A review of the literature and description of the theoretical foundation of the study or educational program is often included as part of the significance section. In some cases it is contained in a separate section. If you are writing a research proposal, it is important to show how the specific aim(s) and research question(s) are supported by a theoretical framework.

Many fields in the human service professions have developed theoretical models to guide practice and curricular development. If your project uses a model or is founded in a particular theoretical approach, it will strengthen your proposal to discuss this framework. A project that is based in theory will significantly advance the body of knowledge in the profession.

Other relevant literature needs to be discussed as well. The review of literature should be comprehensive and yet directly related to the topic of your proposal. It should include only the most pertinent and current works and should not be a long discourse about topics only peripherally related to your project.

There are five major reasons for reviewing the literature (DePoy & Gitlin, 1994). The first is to determine the extent to which your topic has been covered. If your research topic has already been investigated, you need to either reconsider the importance of doing it or modify it significantly to build on the existing literature. If you are considering an educational or demonstration project and it has already been carried out, you might want to modify it in some creative way or apply it to a different population or community.

A second reason for the literature review is to develop the rationale for the importance of your study. Citing other studies that suggest why your study is important or why your educational program would be of value allows you to build a strong case in the significance section of the proposal. It is not redundant to cite certain works in more than one place, although in the literature review section a more thorough discussion is usually required.

The third reason for conducting a literature review is that it will help demonstrate the relevance of your topic to the body of knowledge that exists in a particular area. Fourth, the literature review helps to identify and describe the theoretical foundation of your project. Showing relevance allows you to claim that your study or your program will add to the organized knowledge in a field, and identification of the theoretical framework will show that your project is solidly grounded. Finally, the literature review will help determine the best strategy to use in carrying out your project. Often, reviewing approaches that other investigators have taken can suggest how to best pose a research question and develop the specific design or procedures.

There are several different ways to approach conducting and writing a literature review. Although we recommend the following approach, as suggested by Findley (1989), there is no one best way, and it is often a matter of personal style and comfort.

Start by doing a literature search in your library for articles or research studies that are directly related to the major focus of your project. A good rule of thumb is to review literature that has been published within the past 5 years unless there is an older, "classic" article. Also, be sure to search the literature in fields other than yours. Review the abstracts of the articles and organize them into four categories:

1. Those that appear highly relevant and absolutely essential for you to read for your proposal.
2. Those that are somewhat relevant and will probably be used.
3. Those that are relevant and that you might use.
4. Those that are not relevant.

Begin with the most relevant articles and review them critically. Write down a very brief description of the article or study. If it is a research article, write a four- or five-sentence introduction in which you identify what was studied, how it was studied, what was found, and what conclusions were drawn. Also, discuss any recommendations for future research in these articles that support your own proposed study. If it is not a research article, briefly summarize the major points of the article that are related to your topic. Once you have reviewed the articles in the "most relevant" category, do the same with the articles in the "relevant" category. If the conclusions and/or findings of the articles in these two categories are similar, it is probably time to stop searching for new articles.

There are at least two ways to organize the writing of the literature review. The articles can be presented chronologically, with the oldest articles first, or the articles can be grouped around common themes that are related to your topic. Let's take the example of the educational project for the provision of care to individuals who are homeless. One strategy for reviewing and categorizing the literature is according to articles or studies that:

1. identify national and local statistics about the number of individuals who are homeless;
2. contain demographic data about the homeless population;
3. describe the health care needs of those who are homeless;
4. describe problems faced by those who are homeless in accessing the health care system;
5. discuss the need for new models in delivering health care;
6. discuss the importance of interdisciplinary, community-based health care;
7. discuss the role of each of the nursing and allied health professions in meeting the health care needs of those who are homeless.

In this example, it is fairly obvious that you need to search a number of different bodies of literature to write this section of the proposal. These include studies on team building and collaboration; epidemio-

logical, social work, and sociological research on homeless populations; government research reports; and the literature in each of the
allied health professions that are participating in the project.

In reviewing the literature, it is important to consider resources
outside your own field or profession. Go to the sources in which the
original work in an area was conducted. For example, if you are planning to study a management issue, go to the management literature;
if you are studying an educational issue, look at articles from educational journals that are pertinent to the topic.

If the topic area in which you are interested is one that is not been
studied extensively, your review may be relatively brief. You can then
cite a lack of research as a reason for conducting your study as long
as you have demonstrated that your topic is significant. An important
point to keep in mind is that in your review of the literature you must
always use what are called primary sources. A primary source is the
original article from which an idea comes. It is almost never appropriate to use the discussion of a research article that is presented by an
author who did not do the original study.

At the conclusion of the literature review, provide a summary of
your analysis of the articles. In this concluding section, you might discuss how the findings support your background, significance, research
question, hypotheses, and/or design. Also, identify gaps in knowledge
that the literature review uncovered and how your study or educational
program will fill these gaps.

Once you write this section of the proposal, ask yourself the
questions listed in Box 5.7.

BOX 5.7

SELF-STUDY QUESTIONS

1. Does the literature review present the background
   to the topic of the proposal?
2. Does the literature review critically evaluate and
   synthesize existing knowledge?
3. Are the gaps in knowledge that this study or program will address identified?
4. Does the review provide a basis of support for the
   hypotheses and/or research question?
5. Has the need for the proposed study been documented?
6. Does the literature review appear complete and up
   to date?
7. Is the literature review logically developed?

Methodology/Research or Educational Plan

If you are writing a proposal for a training or demonstration grant, this section will contain a detailed description of each step you will take to carry out your project. This plan of operation must be as carefully developed and as comprehensive as the methodology section of a research proposal. Because you are answering the question about how you will carry out the project, you should organize your description in a step-by-step manner and explain in detail how you will implement the activities necessary to accomplish each objective. Members of a review panel will closely examine your plans for course development and student recruitment. They will also look for whether there is a logical sequence of courses or training experiences and an indication of how your plan complements, improves, or extends existing programs. Consider using flowcharts and tables to describe the curriculum or project design. Graphic displays provide a concise visual summary of your written material and reinforce the major points in the narrative.

If you are planning a research study, the methodology section is critical to the success of your proposal. Each aspect of the research design must be described in detail. In this section, explain to the review panel, in a logical way, each step you plan to take to recruit subjects, and collect and analyze the data. Also describe why you chose the particular research approach or data analysis plan. Important topics to discuss are noted in Box 5.8.

BOX 5.8

SUGGESTED SUBSECTIONS OF RESEARCH METHODOLOGY

1. Overview of design
2. Sample description and selection
3. Procedures and data collection
4. Human subjects
5. Study validity and reliability
6. Assumptions and study limitations
7. Timetable
8. Statistical analysis

If there is a statistician or a department that offers statistical consultation within your institution, you can obtain important help in developing the research design and choosing specific analytic strategies. A statistician may also agree to assist you in writing this section of the proposal in exchange for a paid consultancy to the project if it is funded.

Common mistakes made by applicants in this section include an inadequate justification for why a particular procedure or approach is chosen, poor integration of ideas, incorrect or inappropriate statistical or research design, and a lack of detail about the procedures. These mistakes can be prevented by carefully planning each aspect of the design and by having early drafts reviewed by a research or statistical consultant.

Be aware of one mistake that cannot be corrected and that will lead to disapproval of a proposal, the "fatal flaw." A fatal flaw represents a fundamental problem in the research design that cannot be remedied by simple alterations in the proposal. A design flaw requires a rethinking of the entire project. Box 5.9 presents a comment from a review panel that reflects a fatal flaw in a proposal.

BOX 5.9

EXAMPLE OF A FATAL FLAW

It is difficult to see how this research study, with its proposal cohort design, will adequately test the outcomes of the proposed intervention as it is currently conceptualized. Since random assignment of patients to experimental and control groups would compromise patient treatment plans at this facility, it would be unethical and not feasible to do so. However, without randomization, study outcomes cannot be interpreted in any meaningful way, nor can treatment effectiveness be determined.

Let's examine each subsection of the methodology section in more detail.

Research Design

The research design of a study is the "blueprint," or plan, that describes how the study will be organized, the variables that will be measured, and the data collection and analytic procedures that will be followed (DePoy & Gitlin, 1994). It is important to present a clear and concise description of each component of the research design and to explain why each procedure is the most appropriate for the study.

Begin the research design section with an overview in which you identify and label your design (e.g., a two-group randomized experimental design; regression analysis, 2 x 2 x 2 factorial design) and explain how the design is appropriate to control for variance and threats to validity.

Second, specify the major elements of the design, such as the independent and dependent variables, the sampling frame, sample size and selection procedures, and the number of testing occasions that are planned. It is important to be very specific in your description. For example, when specifying the independent and dependent variables, include how each is related in the study (e.g., causal, explanatory, mediator, predictor). Two examples of design statements are presented in Boxes 5.10 and 5.11.

BOX 5.10

DESIGN STATEMENT 1

This study is designed to evaluate the level of knowledge of case managers in homeless shelters regarding the health care needs of their clients. A descriptive survey design using stratified randomization is proposed in which 100 case managers from 30 homeless shelters in the city of Philadelphia will be randomly selected to complete a questionnaire designed to assess four areas of knowledge: oral hygiene, mental health, drug and alcohol problems, and basic hygiene. The survey will contain demographic information, multiple-choice questions that tap knowledge of signs and symptoms of each problem, and open-ended questions that ask respondents to describe their approach to dealing with each problem.

BOX 5.11

DESIGN STATEMENT 2

The research design chosen for this study is a randomized two-group experimental design to test the effectiveness of a home-based intervention for individuals caring for a family member with dementia. The study involves 250 caregivers who are assigned to either a treatment group or a control group. Subjects in the treatment group receive five home visits by an occupational therapist, whereas those in the control group do not receive any grant-supported services. A 3-month posttest will evaluate the immediate effect of the experimental design to expand caregiver approach to problem solving, ability to identify and introduce environmental modifications, and ability to reduce degree of stress and lessen the frequency of care recipient problem behaviors. A 6-month follow-up interview will assess long-term effects of the program.

After completing the draft of a design statement, ask yourself the questions listed in Box 5.12.

BOX 5.12

SELF-STUDY QUESTIONS

1. Is the research design appropriate to study the research problem?
2. Does the research design control for extraneous variables and threats to validity?

Sample Description and Selection

In this subsection the characteristics of the sample and the procedures by which subjects will be selected for participation in the study are described. The following five basic points should be covered (see also Boxes 5.13 and 5.14):

BOX 5.13

EXAMPLE OF SAMPLE DESCRIPTION 1

Participants in this study will comprise a convenience sample of 250 caregivers, each caring for a family member with moderate dementia. Caregivers who have care recipients with dementia and Parkinson's disease or who are on experimental medication will be excluded from the study. The sample size of 250 is adequate to detect outcomes and is based on a power analysis, with power set at .80, alpha at .05, and an anticipated moderate effect size. No difficulty is anticipated in obtaining a sample of 250 because previous analysis of the five dementia clinics participating in this study report an average of 30 new clients per month for the past 2 years who fit the study criteria.

BOX 5.14

EXAMPLE OF SAMPLE DESCRIPTION 2

This study will comprise a convenience sample of 20 HIV-positive Hispanic men attending an AIDS support group who volunteer to participate in the study. Criteria for eligibility include evidence of HIV-positive test results and a 90% attendance record at support group meetings for the previous 6 months.

Currently, there is an active pool of 50 men who have been tested as HIV-positive. Subject recruitment will occur by two methods. The first method will entail a letter to each active participant, describing the purpose of the study and inviting participation. The second method will entail an explanation of the study by the principal investigator at regular meetings of the support group. Those who agree to participate will be interviewed to determine eligibility.

1. Describe how the sample will be selected. This involves listing criteria for inclusion and exclusion of subjects and the reason for selecting these criteria.
2. Describe the anticipated characteristics of the participants in the study and the extent to which these are representative of

the population to which you plan to generalize the study find-ings. In discussing the sample characteristics, include a descrip-tion of age, gender, race, and health status.

3. Describe the procedures that will be followed to recruit and select the sample.

4. Discuss the sample size and the justification for its adequacy, using power analysis if appropriate.

5. Provide an assurance of the feasibility of obtaining the required sample by giving information such as appropriate characteris-tics of potential participants in the organizations from which you will select the sample.

Once you have a draft of this section, ask yourself the questions in Box 5.15.

BOX 5.15

SELF-STUDY QUESTIONS

1. Is the sample representative of the population of interest?
2. Is the sample size adequate?
3. Is the description of how the sample was derived clearly stated?
4. Is the sampling procedure appropriate (free of sampling error or bias)?
5. Are the procedures described in detail to allow for replication?
6. Is the assignment of subjects to groups appropriate?

Procedures, Materials, or Data Collection Instruments

This subsection should include a discussion of the procedures you will follow and data collection instruments you will use.

First, provide a detailed description of the procedures you intend to implement for data collection. Think about what you need to do if your grant is funded and describe these steps in detail. Box 5.16 pro-vides examples of two discussions of procedures.

Second, discuss the materials that are necessary or the data col-lection instruments that will be used for the study. In describing an instrument, discuss its domains (e.g., demographic information, job satisfaction, psychological stress), the measurement level of a scale,

BOX 5.16

EXAMPLE 1 OF A DISCUSSION OF PROCEDURES

Following notification of grant approval and funding, a letter will be mailed to administrators of participating nursing homes. This letter will explain the purpose of the study and its procedures and the importance of participation of the nursing assistants. The letter will be followed by a telephone call to the administrator to determine an appropriate time to arrange for a 20-minute telephone survey with each nursing assistant. Each participating nursing home will be requested to provide a quiet office setting from which the nursing assistant can participate in the telephone survey.

EXAMPLE 2 OF A DISCUSSION OF PROCEDURES

Cultures will be obtained from 20 HIV-positive patients and identified and quantified on a weekly basis until the infection has been controlled. Thereafter, cultures will be taken monthly for a maximum of 12 months. Treatments will be administered to control the clinical signs and symptoms.

and its validity and reliability for the specific group of subjects included in your study. If you intend to design a data collection instrument, discuss a plan for examining its reliability and obtaining at least face or content validity. Important topics to discuss are noted in Box 5.17, and an example is given in Box 5.18.

BOX 5.17

DATA COLLECTION INSTRUMENTS AND STRATEGIES

1. Describe your data collection instruments.
   • What is their published reliability?
   • What is their published validity?
   • How extensively are they used in other research?
   • Why did you choose these particular instruments?
2. Describe your data collection strategies.
   • How will you collect the data?
   • If you interview subjects, what procedures will you use?

BOX 5.18

EXAMPLE OF A DISCUSSION OF INSTRUMENTATION

The telephone survey will be developed by the investigators and will consist of three primary domains: demographic and background information, items that assess knowledge of oral pathology in the elderly, and a case vignette with questions to determine the ability to recognize signs and symptoms of disease. The survey will be reviewed by five individuals with expertise in oral health care of the elderly. This panel of experts will independently review the survey for its face and content validity. Modifications to the survey instrument will be made on the basis of the panel's review, and the survey will be pilot-tested with five nursing assistants.

Human Subjects

This subsection provides a discussion of the protection of human subjects. The discussion should include (a) your plans to ensure confidentiality of the information or data that you obtain from human subjects, (b) how consent from study participants will be obtained, (c) the potential benefits and risks for a subject associated with participation, and (d) the risk-benefit ratio (see Box 5.19). If you are at a university,

BOX 5.19

EXAMPLE OF DISCUSSION OF HUMAN SUBJECTS

This research is descriptive and involves a telephone survey. Participation in the study will be voluntary, and respondents to the telephone survey will be giving their informed consent to participate. Subject confidentiality will be assured by the use of identification numbers on data sheets. Subject names and other identifying information will be kept in a locked filing cabinet in the office of the investigator and will be separate from the information provided by subjects in response to the survey questions. Information will be reported in aggregate form only, and no participant will be identified.

There are no potential risks to participants. There are no direct personal benefits except for personal satisfaction obtained in participating in research and contributing to building a body of knowledge.

---

your office of research administration should be able to provide assistance in organizing this part of your proposal (see also discussion of the IRB in chapter 4).

Validity and Reliability

In this subsection you need to address both the validity and reliability of your design. Validity refers to whether a design and its procedures are appropriate and will yield information to answer the research question. You should explain the specific procedures designed to assure that your approach is the appropriate way to answer your research question. For example, if your purpose is to demonstrate causality, you would use an experimental design and would discuss why the particular design you chose is most appropriate.

You must also consider the reliability of your approach to data collection and analysis. Clearly describe the specific design features you have established that will assure consistency of procedures in such a way that another investigator could replicate your study. For example, let's say you are obtaining cultures of oral lesions. Discuss the exact procedures you plan to implement to assure that all investigators take cultures from the correct lesion and use the same technique.

Assumptions and Limitations

In this subsection, your discussion should focus on the specific limitations of your design.

Almost every study has some limitations based either on features inherent in the design or on its application to your particular situation. Think about these limitations and how they may introduce possible sources of bias. For example, let's say you are conducting a study using the Delphi technique. The Delphi technique is a method of obtaining consensus on a particular issue from a group of experts. One limitation of this technique is the possibility that some respondents may discuss their opinions with others who they know are participants in the study. This could have consequences for your findings and should be identified; the ways in which you will try to overcome it should also be discussed.

Timetable

Base your start-up date and the length of time that will be required to accomplish the major activities of your study on the earliest possible funding date for your proposal. Then provide a table that summarizes each major activity and the time frame for its completion.

Boxes 5.20 and 5.21 offer two examples of how this material can be presented.

Once you have completed a draft of this section, consider the questions in Box 5.22 as a way of reflecting on your proposal.

BOX 5.20

EXAMPLE 1 OF TIMETABLE

ACTIVITY	TIME FRAME
Questionnaire development	Months 1–3
Pilot-testing of instruments	Month 4
Subject recruitment	Months 5–8
Subject interviewing	Months 5–10
Data entry, data cleaning	Months 10–12
Data analysis	Months 12–15
Report generation	Months 15–18

BOX 5.21

EXAMPLE 2 OF TIMETABLE

Activity	*Timeline*							
	July	Aug.	Sept.	Oct.	Nov.	Dec.	Jan.	Feb.
Instrument development	X	X						
Pilot test of protocol			X					
Sample selection			X					
Mail survey				X				
Reminder notice					X			
Second reminder notice						X		
Data entry and analysis						X	X	
Report writing and dissemination								X

BOX 5.22

SELF-STUDY QUESTIONS

1. Is the design appropriate for the research question and logically developed?
2. Is the instrumentation adequate and its reliability and validity addressed?
3. Is there a timetable of major activities that accurately reflects the requirements of the study design and provides an adequate time frame for each activity?
4. Is the sampling plan appropriate for the research question and adequate to assure sufficient sample size and the required sample?

Statistical Analysis

This section involves a discussion of your analytic strategy and the statistical tests you plan to use. In your discussion, it is helpful to restate the hypotheses of your study and then identify the specific statistical test. Also, provide a brief rationale for your choice of this test and the significance level or alpha that will be used to determine statistical significance.

Be sure that the analyses you select fit the measurement level of your data. For example, if your data are categorical or ordinal, a descriptive and nonparametric statistical approach should be used. Your primary method of presentation would be frequency tables involving distribution of percentages. You may wish to consult with a statistician to determine the best analytic approach for your study. Keep in mind that the analyses you choose are an extension of your study design and must answer the research question. Box 5.23 provides two examples of discussions of statistical designs.

Once you complete your discussion of the statistical analysis, ask yourself the self-study questions in Box 5.24 as a check to see that you have included all of the appropriate material.

BOX 5.23

EXAMPLE 1 OF A DISCUSSION OF STATISTICAL ANALYSIS

The major hypothesis to be tested in this study is that students who participate in a computer-assisted learning experience will demonstrate greater knowledge of oral pathology and greater satisfaction with their educational experience. Analysis of covariance tests (ANCOVA) will be used as the primary statistical analytic strategy to determine experimental effect on the two dependent variables (knowledge of oral pathology and student satisfaction). ANCOVA is the statistical test typically used in a two-group experimental design involving pre- and posttest data.

Also, demographic data obtained from this study will be tabulated by using crosstab frequency distributions and measures of central tendency. All tests of significance will be reported at the .05 level.

EXAMPLE 2 OF A DISCUSSION OF STATISTICAL ANALYSIS

A combination of statistical methods will be used to compare the characteristics of dental hygienists who participate in the mail survey questionnaire. Analysis of categorical variables will involve crosstab frequency distributions with chi-square statistics. Comparisons of the two groups (novice and experienced dental hygienists) on continuous variables will be based on analysis of variance (ANOVA). Significant ANOVAs will be followed up with Tukey's HSD (Honestly Significant Difference) test for multiple comparisons. To determine statistical significance, alpha will be set at .01 to control for Type I error, and all statistical tests will be based on a two-tailed distribution.

BOX 5.24

SELF-STUDY QUESTIONS FOR STATISTICAL SECTION

1. Are the statistical analyses appropriate to answer my research question and to test the proposed hypotheses?
2. Are the statistical analyses appropriate for the measurement level of the data that will be collected?

Dissemination Plan

Most agencies want to assure that their funds are used wisely and that the results of a successful project have a wide impact. From their perspective, it makes little sense to fund a project if only a few people will benefit from a successful outcome. Therefore, many agencies require that you present a systematic plan to show how you will disseminate the results of your project. Two important and commonly accepted ways to do this are through presentations at national, scientific, and professional meetings and publication in professional journals. You should also try to include more creative or innovative ways to ensure a wide distribution of your findings. These methods may include the development and distribution of instructional manuals, plans to develop workshops or continuing education programs, or special ways to reach consumers as well as other professional groups.

Plan of Management

In this section, you begin to answer the question about why you are the most appropriate one to carry out this project. Although you may have a wonderful idea, you must also assure the agency that you can accomplish the program goals efficiently. This question can usually be answered by showing that you have a clear, logical, and efficient plan of management that will be executed by a project team composed of well-qua..._u people at an institution that can provide the necessary support and resources. A clear description of the organizational and management structure will answer the first part of this question. In your management plan, you should discuss in detail the roles and responsibilities of key personnel, the amount of time each person will work on the project, and the time frame in which each project task will be carried out. Agencies frequently request that you organize this information in the form of a time line or a detailed Gantt chart of major activities.

An approach to writing this section is to pretend you have already been funded. Think about exactly what you would have to do to carry out your plan if you started tomorrow. Whom would you need to hire? What contacts would be important? What resources would you need? Logically and rationally think through your plan before you write the section. This process may raise critical points of weakness in your research or curriculum design, or it may highlight limitations in institutional resources.

Investigative Team Credentials

This section also helps answer the question about your qualifications to carry out the project. Review your plan to determine the special skills that are necessary to carry out each step of the project and carefully select team members with this expertise. For example, if you are proposing a study that requires a repeated-measures design or statistical modeling techniques, make sure you have a statistician on your team with expertise in these specific analytic strategies. If your study uses naturalistic inquiry, you will need to assure that a member of your team is an expert in qualitative methodologies and software programs. In writing an educational grant, make sure you are working with someone who has curriculum development skills. Select individuals with complementary experience and credentials. For example, in an educational grant, you might need two people, one with curriculum development skills and one with experience in curriculum evaluation.

In writing about the credentials of the team, you should include a brief descriptive paragraph highlighting the qualifications of each member. Emphasize their past experience, publications or presentations that show expertise in the topic of the project. You should also cite funding for other projects, either from sources external to your institution or from your institution, that you or other members have received. Sometimes offices held in professional organizations, teaching or consulting experiences provide additional credibility and demonstrate that you have the necessary background to implement the project successfully.

Institutional Qualifications

Just as your team needs to be qualified, your institution needs to have the resources to assist and support you in carrying out your project. You will need to include a concise description of your institutional resources and its qualifications. For example, has your institution acquired a significant amount of external funding? Does it have a comprehensive library, a learning resource center, or an active research office? What are the computer facilities that are available for your use?

Budget

This section addresses the cost of your project and why it will cost what it does. You will need to prepare a budget that is not inflated or wasteful but sufficient to accomplish all your activities. Do not try to pad your budget by inflating costs or adding unnecessary expenses. Also, do not underestimate what it will cost. The best rule of thumb is to develop a budget that accurately reflects the cost of the activities you are proposing. Most institutions have budget offices or offices of research administration that can be of help to you as you prepare this budget.

You will also be required to justify each expense. This should be included in a budget justification section following the actual budget. In this section describe what each item will be used for and why it is necessary for your project. We discuss budget preparation in more detail in chapter 6.

References

As in all scientific work, references for your sources of information are required. If the agency does not specify a reference style, use the *Publication Manual of the American Psychological Association.* In all cases be consistent in the presentation of references. Also, be sure to check the instructions to determine if there is a page limitation for this section. For example, the PHS 398 form specifies that no more than six pages of references be included in an application.

Appendix Material

The appendixes usually include information that supplements the narrative. For example, appendix material may include the complete curriculum vitae of key members of the project team, sample questionnaires or evaluation instruments, pertinent articles that you have written that relate to the project, curriculum materials, and, most important, letters of support from consultants, leaders in your profession, or your senators and congresspersons.

Chapter 6

Preparing a Budget

INFORMATION REQUIRED

In preparing a budget for a grant application, there are three considerations: (1) the policies and requirements of the agency from which
grant funds are being sought, (2) the policy and requirements of your
institution, and (3) the resources and costs associated with each project task.

Agency Information

Prior to developing a proposal budget, it is important to learn the types
of activities that an agency will fund as part of the grant program, as
well as the way in which you will be expected to manage the budget if
you should receive the award. Table 6.1 outlines the key questions you
should either ask a project officer or search for the answers to in an
application kit before developing your proposal budget.

First, it is important to learn if there is a limit imposed on the
amount of money that can be requested and whether that limit
includes direct and indirect costs. Box 6.1 contains an example of how
this information is provided in a request for applications (RFA).

TABLE 6.1   Agency Budget Questions

Questions regarding the competition

1. What is the projected average cost of a project that will be funded?
2. What is the maximum that can be asked for a project, and does that reflect direct and indirect costs?
3. What is the allowable indirect cost recovery rate that can be requested?
4. What are the allowable budget object categories for which funds can be requested?

Questions regarding budget management

1. Can funds be carried over from one project year to the next?
2. Is there level funding, or can cost of living increases be requested each project year?
3. Are no-cost extensions granted at the end of the project period to complete grant activities?

BOX 6.1

EXAMPLE OF BUDGET SPECIFICATIONS PROVIDED IN AN RFA

Approximately $2 million is projected to be available in fiscal year 1995 to fund six to nine grants. The amount of funding actually available may vary and is subject to change. New grant awards will not exceed $300,000 per year (including both direct and indirect costs). Grant applications that exceed the $300,000 per year cap will be returned to the investigator as nonresponsive.

Although an agency may not specify the total amount of funds that an investigator can request in a particular competition, it may indicate the anticipated average award. This information is important because it lets you know the scope of the projects the agency is seeking to support. For example, let's say an agency anticipates granting an average of $150,000 per project and this amount includes both the direct costs of the project and the allowable indirect costs. An application whose budget significantly exceeds that amount may be evaluated poorly, or if funded, the grant budget may be cut to bring it into line with the agency's expectations.

Each agency has its own rules about the expenses that are allowed and those that are not. These rules may differ for each competition that is sponsored by a particular agency. For example, a number of professional associations sponsor competitions that do not support a salary for the investigator, graduate student tuition, stipends, travel to professional meetings, or equipment costs. Many requests for applications that are issued by federal agencies do not support costs associated with renovation of existing facilities, equipment, or direct patient care. Therefore, it is very important for you to learn what expenses are allowed.

The indirect cost recovery rate will differ depending on the agency and the particular type of competition. For example, some foundations will allow an 8% or 10% indirect cost rate, whereas others will not allow any indirect cost charges. Most competitions at the federal level will allow an applicant to apply the rate that has been prenegotiated by the institution. The application kit usually specifies the rate that is allowable and any other budget restrictions or guidelines that exist. However, you should also feel free to contact the program officer to inquire about budget questions that you may have.

It is also important to know the rules of an agency for managing budgets of awarded grants. These rules may shape how you develop your budget and will differ among agencies and competitions. For example, some agencies will allow the investigator to take unspent funds in one project year and spend them in the following year. These are called carryover funds. Other agencies will not allow this, so if you don't spend all of your funds during a project year, you will lose them. This has important implications for how you plan the activities of your project. If certain activities are not accomplished before the end of the budget year, there will be no funds to carry them out at a later time.

For example, let's say you receive a 3-year award to conduct a research study in which 150 families with children with a physical disability will be interviewed and observed to examine caregiving issues and developmental patterns. In your original plan, you anticipated recruiting and interviewing 50 families and observing their children in each project year. Therefore, you developed a budget that reflected costs for interviewing and observing 50 families per year. However, during the first year you encounter a number of problems such as slow recruitment and a need for more time to establish interrater reliability of the observation instrument, and you are able to interview and observe only 30 families and children. You will have unspent funds that reflect the costs of interviewing the 20 families who have not yet entered the study. If the agency allows you to carry over these funds, all you need do is adjust your recruitment efforts and increase the number of families in the second year. However, if the agency does not allow carryover funds, you have a problem in that you lose the opportunity to use these funds and must adjust your activities accordingly. Although there are some ways to overcome this limitation, it is best to consult with your institution's business office and the program officer who is monitoring your grant to plan the most appropriate strategy.

It is also important to learn whether the funding agency and the particular competition for which you are applying allow yearly increases for salary and cost of living or whether there is what is called level funding. If an agency allows yearly budget increases, usually 4% to 6% salary increases can be built into the budget. If an agency enforces level funding, then the total budget request for the first project year is the amount that will be awarded in each year of the project.

Level funding has very important implications for how you plan the flow of project activities. With level funding it is important to distribute activities evenly over the years of the project. For example, let's say you are planning an education program for students in allied health. Your first year involves a long start-up period and significant coordination and planning activities. Your budget will therefore be modest because these are relatively inexpensive activities. However, if in your second year you actively recruit 40 students and hire three new faculty members and two new clinical supervisors to instruct in the new courses that are developed, your budget will be significantly higher. If the agency allows budgets to fluctuate from year to year, this approach to the project would pose few problems. However, if level funding is required, this approach would seriously jeopardize your ability to carry out the project because you could receive only the amount of funds you requested for project year 1.

Most agencies will allow "no-cost extensions." In a no-cost extension an investigator is allowed to extend the life of the grant beyond its funded period by using any unspent funds from the final year to complete the project activities. This flexibility is especially important in research grants wherein many activities, such as subject recruitment and interviewing, can be delayed due to circumstances that are beyond the control of the investigator. Once again, be on the safe side and call the program officer to be sure that no-cost extensions are allowed. Although it is important to know whether an agency allows a no-cost extension, this should have little immediate effect on how you plan the budget for your proposal submission.

Institution-Related Information

A second important consideration in preparing a grant budget is the specific requirements that have been established by your institution. For example, you will need to conform to your institution's personnel salary scale and apply the institutional rate for fringe benefits and indirect cost recovery. Table 6.2 lists the six questions you need to ask an official in your institution prior to developing and submitting a proposal budget. Depending on the organization structure of your institution, you will obtain this information from either the office of the controller, the office of the budget administrator, the office of research administration, or the office of sponsored programs.

Most institutions develop a set of procedures for reviewing the budgets of proposals to ensure that they conform to the institution's requirements. Some large universities will develop the budget for an investigator.

Project Cost Considerations

Finally, in developing a budget for a proposal, you need to estimate carefully the cost of each project task, then develop a budget that is realistic and reflects the financial support needed for the study. That is, your budget should reflect what you actually need and not what would be nice to have. It should also use and build on the resources of your institution. For example, although it would be nice to have a full-time secretary on your project, most do not require this level of support. Therefore, it would be inappropriate to request a 100% secretarial position when only a 30% effort is actually required. By building on the resources at your institution, you may be able to increase the time of

TABLE 6.2   Institution-Related Budget Considerations

1. What is the institution's fringe benefit rate?
2. What is the institution's allowable yearly percentage of merit or inflationary salary increase?
3. What is the institution's indirect cost recovery rate?
4. What is the accepted salary for key personnel who must be hired?
5. What is the institution's rate for car travel reimbursement?
6. What will the institution permit as in-kind contributions?

a part-time secretary or renegotiate the role of a full-time secretary so that 30% of his or her effort will be devoted to your project.

Budget considerations will also influence the design of the project and its scope. The budget you request should accurately reflect the costs associated with each project activity. Therefore, you need to think about the budget as you develop your program to ensure that you can accomplish your project with the amount of money available to you.

As you develop the budget, ask yourself the questions in Table 6.3 as a guide.

TABLE 6.3   Self-Study Questions for Budget Development

1. Is my budget practical and realistic for the tasks I plan to accomplish?
2. Is my budget appropriate for the tasks I need to accomplish, my level of resources, and the costs allowable by the agency?
3. Are the grant funds I am requesting sufficient to offset the costs of my project?
4. Is my budget comprehensive in that it covers all costs associated with the implementation of my project?

BASIC COMPONENTS

There are usually three major components of a proposal budget: (1) direct costs, (2) indirect cost allowances, and (3) institutional commitments. Each of these is discussed here in detail.

Direct Costs

Direct costs are those that are necessary to carry out your project. The following eight budget categories are accepted by the Public Health Service; however, most of these categories are similar to those requested by other federal agencies and foundations.

Personnel

This category refers to the salary support requested for each member of the project team. The project team usually includes the principal investigator, project director or coordinator, interviewers, research assistants, secretary, and other personnel who may participate in the development and implementation of the project. Starting with the principal investigator, list the names and identify the roles of all the people who will be involved on the project during the budget period. In this section, list only those who are employees of your institution or who will be hired by the institution to work on the grant. To determine the cost of these salaries, first estimate the amount of time each person will spend on the project. Usually, this time is calculated as a percentage of a person's full-time job commitment. Next, multiply this percentage by an individual's base annual salary. If the person is on a 9- or 10-month employment contract and is asked to work on the grant during the summer months, a separate calculation for the summer salary will be required. The next step is to compute the cost of fringe benefits attributable to this salary, a rate determined by your institution. These two figures are then added to determine the person's salary paid for by the grant. Box 6.2 provides an example of how you would compute a salary line.

Similar calculations are made for all members of the project team.

BOX 6.2

EXAMPLE OF SALARY CALCULATION

Dr. J. is an assistant professor of physical therapy with a 10-month salary of $35,000. She has been included as a faculty member in an application for a training grant that the department is submitting. The principal investigator, Dr. M., has determined that she will need 10% of Dr. J.'s time during the academic year and 1 full month during the summer. The university fringe benefit rate is 26.5%. Dr. M. computes her salary line in the following manner. First, she takes 10% of $35,000, or $3,500. This is Dr. J.'s salary covered by the grant during the academic year. Dr. M. then computes her benefit allowance by multiplying $3,500 by 26.5%, or $928. This is the fringe benefit cost rounded to the nearest whole dollar. The fringe benefit cost is added to the salary ($3,500 + $928 = $4,428) to determine the total grant contribution to Dr. J.'s salary during the academic year. Dr. J. will also work for 1 month during the summer, which requires a separate calculation. As Dr. J. is on a 10-month contract, her monthly salary is $3,500 ($35,000 x 10%), and her fringe benefit rate will be $928 (26.5% x $3,500). Therefore, her summer compensation will be $4,428 ($3,500 + $928).

Consultants

Consultants are individuals who are not university employees but who will work on your project. For example, on a research grant you might require the assistance of a statistician to analyze your data. On a training grant you may need to consult with a recognized expert on the content of your project. You will need to negotiate the compensation for these individuals and report it in the nonsalary section of the budget. Fringe benefits are not calculated for consultant fees. However, a consultant may request an amount that includes his or her own institution's benefit rate.

Equipment

Items such as furniture or equipment that have a usable life of 2 or more years and cost over $500 are reported in this section. Computers, slide projectors, fax machines, and special laboratory equipment fall into this category. The full cost of these should be reported. A word of caution is in order here. You should request funding only for equipment that is essential to your project and not already available at your institution. Because equipment may last longer than the life of your grant, review panels and funding agencies will study this category closely to assure that you are not unnecessarily "padding your budget" to purchase items you may need in your department. For example, a few years ago personal computers were not common in faculty offices or laboratories, and many investigators purchased them with grant funds. Today the purchase of personal computers for employees is often considered the responsibility of the institution, and funding agencies are less willing to support their purchase. Money for items such as slide projectors are rarely approved, also because agencies consider the purchase of such equipment as the responsibility of your institution. To obtain approval for the purchase of durable, fixed equipment, you must provide a strong justification for its importance to your project and a rationale as to why the funding agency, rather than your institution, should support the cost.

Supplies

These include daily office needs such as stationery, audiotapes, pencils and paper, and laboratory supplies such as reagents and chemicals that are necessary for your project. Funding agencies are usually more flexible in approving these items. Often there is no need to itemize supplies if your total request is less than $1,000. But, like equipment, if an agency wants to cut your budget, supplies are an easy target. As with all proposed purchases, estimate as closely as you can the cost of all the materials you will need and ask for that amount with a justification for the expenditure.

Trainee Expenses

This category is usually found only in applications for training grants. All costs related to individuals, usually students, who will be the recipients of the training provided by the grant are included in this section. These include expenses such as tuition, stipends, travel, or other costs associated with supporting the participation of trainees in your project.

Travel

Travel expenses include all forms of transportation, lodging, meals, meeting registration fees, and incidental expenses associated with travel by key project personnel for project-related activities. Travel costs must be associated with the specific needs of your project. They may include travel to attend a conference to present a paper that disseminates project results, attend meetings to interact with other professionals who have knowledge related to the content of your project, attend meetings related to your project, interview subjects in a study, and convene an advisory board to review your project. You should request only clearly justifiable travel expenses and provide an estimate of hotel and transportation costs. Also, each institution uses an adjusted government rate for reimbursing travel by car. For example, the current government rate is $0.31 a mile, but inquire about the rate used by your institution.

Alterations and Renovations

In some cases, agencies will fund alterations or renovations to a physical space if they are necessary to implement your project. For example, if you are conducting a study of wheelchair access, you may be able to receive funding for renovations to install ramps or widen doorways. Costs for space rental are usually not allowable because these costs are included in the indirect cost recovery rate that your institution is legally permitted to request. Some foundations provide support for major construction projects such as the erection of a building. However, these "bricks and mortar" projects are becoming less common. For most beginning investigators, alterations and renovations will not be relevant budget items.

Consortium/Contractual Costs

There may be situations in which you will need to work with another agency or institution: a school of allied health may want to collaborate with a school of education to conduct an educational training project, a department of laboratory sciences might want to work with an equipment company in a study of new technology, or a department of occupational therapy might want to develop an agreement with a rehabilitation hospital to study a particular therapeutic intervention. These types of arrangements require special agreements between the participating institutions.

The two most common arrangements are consortial and contractual agreements. In a consortial arrangement both parties will have responsibility for the scope of the entire project, although each will carry out different aspects. However, one institution will be required to serve as the principal institution and oversee the receipt and disbursement of funds. Another approach would be to contract with another institution for specific services. In such an arrangement you would effectively be purchasing these services from the other institution. In either of these arrangements all participating institutions will have their own rules regarding compensation of personnel, allowable costs, and overhead rates. Your institution may have standard forms and specific procedures for entering into contractual or consortial agreements. When contemplating either, you should refer to your institution's office of research administration.

Assuming that your institution will be the lead or principal institution in a consortial or contractual arrangement, your organization will receive and disburse all funds. The participating institution will then disburse these monies internally. Be certain that you have reached a clear agreement about the exact services to be provided, notification of their completion, and a schedule of payments. There are also important considerations regarding indirect costs in these arrangements, which will be discussed in the following pages.

"Other" Expenses

All expenses not specifically covered in other categories are reported in this section. These can include miscellaneous expenses such as lunch for an advisory board, long-distance telephone costs, data entry and computer costs, or payments to subjects. For example, a project involving pediatric AIDS might include money in the budget for small gifts for the children as a way of encouraging participation and showing appreciation for a family's involvement.

Indirect Costs

Because you will occupy institutional space for your project, government agencies and foundations have agreed to help defray these costs. These are called indirect costs and represent a reimbursement to your university or agency for their costs associated with your research or training project, such as building maintenance, utilities, insurance, and other general administrative expenses. An allowance for indirect or overhead expenses is based on a set rate or a prenegotiated percentage of certain direct costs of the grant.

Overhead or indirect cost recovery rates for research grants vary widely. In many cases this allowance is negotiated in advance between the university and a federal agency. For some agencies, such as the National Institutes of Health, the indirect rate may range from 60% to 80% of modified total direct costs. This rate is added to the total funding allowance for the grant when you submit your proposal. Other agencies, such as the U.S. Department of Education, do not have a standard negotiated rate for research projects. An institution must propose an indirect cost recovery rate that, when added to the direct costs, falls within a budget range acceptable to the agency.

Training grants have overhead rates different from those of research grants because most expenses are in the form of tuition and stipend payments to students. These and other related training activities usually do not directly use additional university resources. Therefore, the federal government uses a smaller indirect cost recovery rate, usually 8%.

How do you calculate the indirect costs for your project? Not all expenses in your proposal can be used to compute your indirect cost recovery. This allowance is based on what is called a modified direct cost amount. The general rule of thumb is that any expense in your grant involving university facilities or resources is used as a basis to compute the modified direct costs. These include the expenses found in the following categories: personnel, travel, supplies, consultants, and "other." Equipment purchases, trainee expenses over $500, and consortial and contractual costs are not allowable as part of the indirect cost base because none of these involve the resources of your institution. In computing your indirect cost recovery, add the amounts in each of the allowable categories and multiply that amount by either 8% for a training grant or the negotiated rate of your institution for other types of projects. Simply add this amount to the total of the direct costs of your project to calculate the total costs. If your institution does not have a negotiated rate with the funding agency to which you are applying, you should discuss the most appropriate rate with your budget administrator or office of research administration. When you enter into an arrangement with another institution, their indirect cost recovery is included in the total amount of money that you agree to pay them, so separate calculations are not necessary.

Institutional Commitments

An agency or a foundation often requests that an institution contribute in some way to the financing of a project. This can be done in several ways. First, an institution can contribute time for members of the project team. For example, if you estimate that a 40% effort is required by a member of your team, your institution may agree to donate 10% and ask the granting agency to pay 30%. Box 6.3 provides an example of how this might be done.

BOX 6.3

EXAMPLE OF INSTITUTIONAL COMMITMENT

Dr. K. is a member of a project team that involves a consortial arrangement between two universities. One of his administrative responsibilities is to encourage external relationships between his university and other agencies. Because the project requires a research or administrative liaison between the two universities, 10% of Dr. K.'s time is donated to the project for that purpose. Because this role is legitimately part of the grant activity and his daily responsibilities, it is an appropriate university contribution to the project.

An alternative way to demonstrate university commitment is through a waiver of a portion of the indirect cost recovery allowance. If your university has a negotiated indirect cost rate of 67% with an agency such as NIH, you might request a lower rate, such as 50%, and show the difference (17%) as a university contribution. If you are applying to an agency in which there is no negotiated indirect cost rate, you could still use the 67% rate as a baseline to demonstrate an in-kind contribution.

A third way to demonstrate commitment is through the donation of supplies or mailing, phone, or duplicating expenses. For example, some universities have centralized mailing or purchasing systems, with the costs for mailing and supplies distributed throughout the university. For small mailings and limited supply purchases, the university might agree to share these costs with the granting agency.

These are all examples of legitimate cost-sharing expenses. In developing a budget, be certain that your institution is agreeable to the in-kind commitments you include in the costs of your project. Most institutions are as concerned with the financial implications of a project as they are with its scientific integrity. Consequently, they typically have rules about what costs should be covered in a grant proposal budget. For example, some colleges and universities may allow you to offer clerical or secretarial support or basic office supplies as an in-kind contribution. Others will require that you request the granting agency to cover these expenses. Many institutions will have an office of research administration that is charged with overseeing all grants submitted by employees of the institution. You should check with this office prior to developing your budget. Not only will they be familiar with the rules of your institution, but they can often help you develop a realistic and adequate budget. Cost-sharing commitments can have an effect on faculty and administrative workload, and institutions have different policies related to the kinds and value of services they are willing to commit.

Box 6.4 provides an example of a budget that shows in-kind contributions and related budget items.

BUDGET JUSTIFICATION

You are also required to provide a detailed justification for each expense of the project. A budget justification involves a brief explana-

BOX 6.4

Example of a Budget

Personnel

Position on project	% Effort	Salary Requested	Fringe (.265)	In-kind	Grant Requested Funds
Investigator	30	$14,400	$3,816	$18,216	
Research assistant	10	1,800	477		$2,277
Secretary	10	2,000	530		2,530
Subtotals:		18,200	4,823	18,216	4,807

Consultants
Questionnaire design (10 hr x $40)	$400
Statistical support (5 hr x $40)	200

Supplies
Business envelopes (50 x 4 mailings .01)	2
Diskettes	20
Postage, printing costs, duplication	1,000

Travel
Parking for meetings at collaborative sites	100

Other
Data entry and computer costs	500

Total direct project costs	$19,216	$6,029

tion and rationale for each line item in the budget. In writing the justification, start with "Personnel" and describe each person's roles and responsibilities on the project and provide a rationale for their percentage effort. Then, systematically explain each line item of the budget and demonstrate how each cost is derived. Box 6.5 illustrates an excerpt from a budget justification.

BOX 6.5

EXAMPLE OF A BUDGET JUSTIFICATION FOR PERSONNEL

Personnel: The university will provide in-kind support in the form of salary and benefit support for the investigator, who will commit 30% effort to this project. Grant funds are being requested for a project secretary who will provide clerical support and coordinate the printing and mailings of the survey. This individual will devote 10% of her time to this project. Funds are also requested for a research assistant who will devote 10% effort to this project.

Chapter 7

Technical Considerations

Knowledge of the technical aspects of writing a proposal can improve the competitiveness of your submission. These include writing a concept paper, obtaining supporting documentation by conducting needs assessments or pilot studies, and attending to administrative matters. In this chapter we examine some of the common practices in grant writing that are learned through experience.

ELEMENTS OF A CONCEPT PAPER

Developing a concept paper before writing a full proposal is a strategy that many individuals find useful. A concept paper is similar to an extended abstract or an executive summary in that it outlines the major elements of the project you are thinking of developing. It is a brief document, comparable to a miniproposal, containing many of the important elements of a full proposal. The concept paper is a very flexible tool in that it can help guide your proposal writing, can be shared with multiple funding agencies, and will allow you to receive feedback from a variety of sources. The key to a well-written concept paper is to

TABLE 7.1 Elements of a Concept Paper

1. Statement of problem and rationale
2. Research question or objectives
3. Methodology
4. Estimated budget requirements (not essential)
5. Key personnel

provide important information without burdening the reader with every detail that needs to be included in a full proposal. The Agency for Health Care Policy and Research (AHCPR) recommends that a concept paper be 6 to 10 double-spaced pages; other agencies recommend 3 to 5 double-spaced pages. In either case, the concept paper usually contains five basic sections, as shown in Table 7.1. As you can see, these sections parallel many of the sections in a full proposal.

The first section of a concept paper provides an introductory paragraph that describes the problem you plan to address and explains its importance or significance. Although you may wish to cite literature, only a brief reference list of key citations should be included. This is followed by a brief explanation of the specific aims or the short- and long-term objectives of the project and a description of the methodology you plan to use to attain the objectives. In a research project, you would include a statement about the design, sampling procedures, sample size, measures, and data collection techniques. You may then wish to include a statement about the estimated budget requirements for the project with a brief justification of overall project costs. Although some agencies may not be interested in detailed budget information at this stage, others may find an overall cost estimate helpful in evaluating whether your plan is feasible and consistent with the agency's funding levels. Finally, you will need to indicate the key participants in the project and their respective areas of expertise.

It may initially appear that writing a concept paper is unnecessary or a waste of time because its elements reflect the basic components of a grant application. However, taking the time to write such a paper has certain benefits, especially for a new investigator. Five major uses of a concept paper are summarized in Table 7.2. First, some federal agencies may require a written statement of your intentions prior to submitting a full grant application. They may ask for either a "letter of intent," which is simply a letter stating your intent to submit to a particular competition, or a more developed set of ideas in

TABLE 7.2   Uses of a Concept Paper

1. Discussion with federal project officers
2. Submission to a foundation to determine interest
3. Obtaining feedback from colleagues
4. Advancing efforts of the grant-writing team
5. Working draft to assist in writing the grant proposal

the form of a concept paper. Even if a concept paper is not required, it is advantageous to send one to a project officer a few months in advance of the deadline for a particular competition in order to obtain specific feedback. Project officers in most federal agencies will read and comment on such documents if they receive them at least 1 month prior to the due date of a competition. However, be sure to call the agency first to determine their policy on reading and commenting on proposal ideas. Furthermore, if you plan to meet with a project officer, sending a concept paper prior to your meeting allows the project officer time to think about your ideas; then you can both use your meeting time more effectively.

Second, the concept paper can be used with project officers at foundations or with corporate leaders. Sending a concept paper with an introductory letter is often the desired approach to many foundations. You may also send the paper to more than one foundation or corporation simultaneously, which will save you time in determining where there may be interest in your idea.

Third, the concept paper offers a way to obtain feedback from your colleagues. Because it is a brief document, it is not too time-consuming to read. And because it captures the essence of your project, it will enable you to obtain meaningful advice and suggestions without placing a burden on those who read it.

Fourth, the concept paper is an effective way to foster the efforts of a work team responsible for a grant submission. The paper, as a reflection of the current thinking of the group, allows an opportunity for review and refinement and helps the group formulate the next steps in developing the grant application.

Fifth, because the concept paper contains the basic elements of the actual grant application, it serves as the first working draft of the proposal. It can also be shared with individuals who intend to write letters of support for the application. Finally, aspects of the concept paper can be used to develop a submission to the institutional review board if human subjects are involved.

NEEDS ASSESSMENTS AND PILOT EFFORTS

In chapter 5 we emphasized the importance of demonstrating the significance of your idea and your familiarity with the field of inquiry. An important way of demonstrating both points is to conduct a pilot study and present your findings in a section of the proposal designated as either "Background and Significance," "Preliminary," or "Pilot Efforts."

The submission of an application for a demonstration, training, or education project usually requires that its significance be adequately demonstrated by a *needs assessment.* A needs assessment is a systematic approach for defining, analyzing, and evaluating a problem so that an intervention or plan of action, such as an education program, can be developed that targets that need. A needs assessment provides data that define the nature and scope of the problem, identify the target population, and ensure that a project is relevant.

For example, let's say you are proposing a continuing education program to advance the ability of practicing health professionals, such as occupational therapists and physical therapists, to provide family-centered care in early intervention programs in your region. To substantiate the need for such a program and its significance for improving services, it would be important to survey systematically the major early intervention programs in a designated geographic region. Such an assessment might include the following:

1. The number of health professionals in the region who are currently providing services.

2. The number of families currently receiving services.

3. The number of families on waiting lists for services.

4. The education level of practicing health professionals.

5. The level of knowledge in family-centered approaches to care.

6. The number of practitioners who would participate in a continuing education program to advance their practice.

7. The number and type of educational opportunities in the region that are similar to the program you are proposing.

The numeric data that would be obtained from this data collection effort may provide evidence of personnel shortages, lack of knowledge of family-centered care strategies by practitioners in the current system, and the need for continuing education programs. This evidence would be important to substantiate the need for a proposed continuing education program.

There are a range of methodological strategies that can be used to conduct a needs assessment. As in other types of research, the selection of a particular methodological approach for a needs assessment must fit the specific purpose, nature of the target population, and resources of the investigator. Table 7.3 describes a few of the methodological approaches that are commonly used to conduct a needs assessment.

Let's say you want to conduct an assessment of the need for an early intervention training program but you are limited in time, financial resources, and personnel to assist in the data collection effort. In such a case, which may be typical when responding to a request for

TABLE 7.3　Methodological Approaches Used in Needs Assessments

Method	Description
Delphi	Mail surveys to reach consensus about an issue from experts. Each expert indicates importance of items along a Likert-type scale through a number of iterations.
Focus groups	Six to 15 individuals with similar backgrounds or experience are brought together to identify or discuss issues in a group. Types of focus groups include key informants, brainstorming, nominal group, and the use of either structured or semistructured questions.
Interviews	Personal, face-to-face interviews using either structured, standardized questions, or open-ended qualitative probes
Mail surveys	Questionnaires sent by mail to a target population
Telephone surveys	Telephone interviews with a target population
Document review	Systematic review of literature, medical records, or other documents
Direct observation	Systematic observations of settings and behaviors

applications, either a telephone interview or a mail survey of administrators of early intervention programs could be used to obtain the necessary data quickly and with limited resources. If time and personnel are not a barrier, however, other methodologies could be considered. For example, a comprehensive survey of therapists, administrators, and family members could be conducted. This approach could be complemented by systematic observation of select treatment sessions to evaluate the extent to which family-centered principles are integrated in practice. Another approach might involve conducting in-depth interviews with families to document their perceptions of the care they receive.

The submission of a grant application for a research study will require the inclusion of data collected as part of one or more pilot studies. There are four major reasons for conducting a pilot study prior to the submission of a research application. As shown in Table 7.4, a pilot study provides an important opportunity to test aspects of a research protocol and obtain information about the target population.

Pilot data can also be used to demonstrate the potential significance of the project and enable the investigator to demonstrate his or her knowledge of the field of inquiry.

Beginning investigators may feel frustrated about the need to obtain pilot data because such efforts often require some level of funding or expenditure of resources. However, it is very important for beginning investigators to obtain preliminary data and develop a track record. Support for small research projects can be obtained from intramural competitions or department or institutional operating budgets. Investigators with a track record who have received prior funding for a research study are able to use the findings from these previous efforts as a basis for proposing a related research project. Obtaining pilot data does not have to be a costly activity. Collaborating with other researchers and conducting a mail survey, selected observations, focus groups, or in-depth interviews are cost-effective strategies from which you can

TABLE 7.4   Reasons for Conducting a Pilot Study

1. To demonstrate investigator's ability to conduct proposed effort and familiarity with area.
2. To pretest feasibility of design or other aspects of methodology.
3. To provide baseline data or preliminary information to justify the proposed effort and its significance.
4. To increase knowledge regarding the area of investigation.

either examine a clearly defined research question or test one aspect of the research protocol for which you are seeking funding.

In presenting preliminary findings, it is important to indicate the way the pilot data supports the need for the study that is being proposed. Box 7.1 provides an excerpt from a grant application that illustrates how to report pilot findings.

BOX 7.1

PRELIMINARY STUDIES

The proposed research builds on and significantly expands the previous research efforts of the investigators. Three studies in particular support the direction of the proposed effort and indicate the potential value of such research.

Study 1: Dementia Management Study

The first study involved a two-group randomized design by which 220 caregivers of individuals with dementia were assigned to either a treatment or control group. Preliminary findings from 110 caregivers who completed the intervention indicate that caregivers requested occupational therapy (OT) intervention for an average of three caregiving problems. A total of 488 environmental strategies were suggested by the occupational therapist during the course of the five home visit interventions. Occupational therapists observed that caregivers were using, on average, 83%, or 406, of these strategies by the end of the intervention period.

These preliminary findings suggest that caregivers can learn and adapt environmental strategies to fit their care situation and respond favorably to a home intervention that addresses individualized need. The intervention proposed in this application builds on and significantly expands the one in this study. The proposed intervention uses the environmental strategies that were developed in this study but tests their effectiveness with caregivers of individuals with multiple sclerosis.

OBTAINING CONTRACTUAL ARRANGEMENTS AND LETTERS OF SUPPORT

In addition to the narrative portion of the grant, other supplementary material should be included in a proposal. For example, if you plan to have a formal work arrangement with another institution, you must sign a legal agreement in the form of a contract with that institution that clearly describes the working arrangement. If your project requires a less formal arrangement or if there are individuals or groups whose participation or endorsement would be required or helpful, letters of support should be included with your proposal.

Contracts are usually handled by your institution. Most institutions have standard forms that have been approved by institutional attorneys and that you must use. If you are at a university, check with your office of research administration for these forms and for help in their completion. If you are at another type of institution or agency, ask your director about the correct procedure to follow. Be sure to specify in the contract all agreements that you have made with the other institution. These include the amount of money that will be paid, the payment schedule, the specific tasks that each party must complete in return for the money, and the time frame for completion of each task. Most institutions will require the legal department or head administrator to review and countersign.

Letters of support are less formal documents with fewer legal implications. However, they are still very important because they help make the argument that you will be able to carry out the project. For example, let's say you are submitting a proposal that involves working with organizations that serve the homeless community. Letters of support from the administrators of homeless shelters, managers in the city government dealing with the homeless population, and other leaders in this area would be essential. In these letters you want to assure the funding agency that you have access to key resources, such as subjects, or the endorsement of individuals or agencies that would be knowledgeable about your project and important for its success. These letters are usually requested personally by a member of the project team. The concept paper can be sent to individuals asked to write a letter of support so that they have the information they need to write the letter.

Both contracts and letters of support can and should be obtained as early in the proposal process as possible. Have one member of the team be responsible for acquiring these while other sections of the proposal are being written. These letters and contracts are placed in one of the appendixes of the final proposal and can be referred to in the document. A letter of support is usually addressed to the project director or principal investigator. It also includes a reference to the title of the project and the name and reference number of the competition.

ADMINISTRATIVE MATTERS

There are other administrative matters that need your attention when submitting a grant. Advance knowledge of these matters can save you time when you write the proposal and in some cases improve your chances of getting funded.

Boilerplate Material

Proposal writing is a very time-consuming activity. Developing a competitive idea, writing the proposal, and doing all the related tasks takes considerable time that must be anticipated. One way of cutting down on time is to prepare in advance the basic information that is required in most proposals. This information is called boilerplate material because it can be used in most grant submissions. Examples of this material are descriptions of your institution's qualifications, biographical sketches of project personnel, and other resources that you have available. Such materials can be prepared in advance and updated when necessary.

The section on institutional qualifications usually includes a series of brief paragraphs that contain a general description of the organization and mission of your institution, agency, college, school, or department. It also includes a description of resources, such as the library, computer facilities, laboratories, institutional or agency affiliations, or any other components that make your organization special or demonstrate that the support you need for the success of the project is available. Most of this information can be found in your university catalog, annual report, or other public information developed by your agency. Consider developing two versions of this material, one relatively brief and another containing much more detail. Either one can then be used, with some modification, in a grant proposal, depending on the depth to which the resources are to be presented. Having the basic framework completed for this section of a grant will save you considerable time and effort.

The description of the qualifications of potential project team members is another example of boilerplate material that can be prepared in advance. Ask members of your department or agency to write two biographical sketches, one long and one short. The long version need not be more than about three paragraphs and should contain a summary of major accomplishments in research, teaching, and service. The short version can be a one-paragraph description of these accomplishments. Activities that can be cited in either version include previously funded grants, major publications, professional recognition and awards, teaching and/or administrative experience, and other special skills. As with the institutional qualifications, you will have to modify this sketch for each proposal to match the most appropriate skills of your team members to a particular project or to the forms required by different agencies. However, advance preparation of the basic content will facilitate your grant-writing effort.

Typing the Proposal

When you write your proposal, make it pleasing to the eye and easy to read. If you have a page limitation, as most proposals do, avoid cramming extra information into the narrative by expanding your margins or using a smaller typeface. Most likely, this extra information is unnecessary. Whatever advantage you may think you gain by its inclusion may be lost by the fatigue and eyestrain experienced in reading your proposal. An attractive, organized, professional-looking proposal enables a review panel to evaluate its content efficiently. Because most proposal writers have access to personal computers and laser jet printers that allow great flexibility in formating and typeface, there is no excuse for submitting a sloppy proposal. Make sure that the printing is clear and crisp, the tables and graphs attractive and easy to read, and the punctuation, spacing, and headings logically consistent. Your proposal should be inviting to read. However, this does not imply that you should use colored graphs or fancy script. Colored graphs, when duplicated, will be black and white. Fancy script may hurt a reviewer's eyes after the first page. Do not right-justify your narrative. Right justification leaves too much white space and is more time consuming to read. Don't waste the reviewer's time and energy.

Duplicating Materials

Most agencies require that you submit the original proposal and anywhere from two to eight copies. These copies must be complete and include all appendixes and attachments. Sometimes agencies need more copies than are required by law. Agencies are on tight budgets, and by sending extra copies you may save your program officer or one of the secretaries time and money. Contact the program officer to inquire how many copies the agency would prefer that you send. Don't forget that duplicating and collating these copies can take time, so plan accordingly.

Duplicating an application is more time-consuming than you may think. Consider completing the appendixes several days prior to the due date. This will allow you to duplicate these materials and eliminate the last-minute rush and stress.

Requesting a Special Review

If you believe that the nature of your proposal requires specific technical expertise, you can request that an individual with this expertise read your proposal as part of the review panel. This request can be made in a cover letter, and the program officer will make a decision regarding its appropriateness.

If you are submitting an application to a federal agency, you can also request that another agency, in addition to the one to which it is submitted, review your proposal. In other words, if you submit a proposal related to aging to the Agency for Health Care Policy and Research, you could also request that the National Institute on Aging review the same proposal. In the NIH, these requests go to a referral officer who can make that decision.

Mailing/Delivering the Proposal

Once you have finished your proposal, it must be delivered to the agency on or before the published due date. The date the submission is due is specified in the general or supplemental instructions, along with the name and address of the office to which the proposal should be delivered and the number of copies to include. In the Department of Education, proposals must be postmarked on or before the due date. Some agencies in the Public Health Service, such as the Bureau of Health Professions, also follow this procedure. Other agencies, such as the NIH, require that the proposals arrive in the Division of Research Grants on or before the due date.

Extensions on deadlines are *never* given. Therefore, pay close attention to the due date and determine the best method of delivery. If, in writing the grant, you see that you will need up to the last minute possible for its completion, you may want to consider sending your proposal by a next-day mail delivery service. Make sure that you obtain a receipt from the post office or courier that clearly shows the date and time of mailing. If your proposal is lost, this receipt is proof, acceptable to the federal government and most foundations, that it was mailed on time. You may also deliver your proposal personally. Investigators in institutions that are close to Washington, DC, or the agency address will often hand-deliver the application. However, as long as the application arrives on time, there is no advantage to either method of delivery.

If You Find a Mistake

After submitting your application, you may discover that you inadvertently neglected to include a particular appendix or that in duplication the ordering of the document was disturbed. These kinds of errors are considered "small," and most agencies will correct them on notification. Call the project officer to indicate the problem and to determine the best course of action.

Plan for a Resubmission

Few proposals are funded on the first submission. Therefore, plan on submitting your proposal more than once. In resubmitting, listen to the advice of your program officer and be responsive to the suggestions of the review panel. (We discuss resubmitting your proposal in more detail in chapter 11.)

Chapter 8

Strategies for Effective Writing

Well-written proposals, those that are clear, focused, and precise, have a greater chance of receiving a favorable review than those that are disorganized, unclear, and filled with typographical errors. Fortunately or unfortunately, the way you write your proposal and present your ideas sends a message to a review panel. High-quality writing and an eye-pleasing presentation send a message that you are conscientious and that your ideas are important and have been carefully developed. Writing that is imprecise and rambling or a presentation that is difficult to follow can make it hard to understand your reasoning and raise doubts about your ability to implement the project. Important ideas and points may be misunderstood, overlooked, or missed.

Although excellent writing will not overcome a poor idea, it will help you sell a good one. However, a poorly written or presented proposal has the potential to hurt the funding chances of a good idea.

As you engage in proposal writing, it is important to understand three points about writing of any kind.

1. Although many people like to have written, few like to write. Writing is hard work. The old adage that good reading is hard writing is true. Writing, like any other skill, takes practice and usually can be improved only by more writing. As you write, rewrite, and write again one or more proposals, you will see improvement in your style.

2. Writing is a very idiosyncratic process. Each person has a particular writing style and a preferred work method. As you continue to write proposals, you will evolve and refine your own preferred approach to the task.

3. Writing takes time. There are no shortcuts. You have to make the time to write. Few people can squeeze writing into a few moments here and there. This is an important point to keep in mind because proposals must be submitted by a specified date. Therefore, you need to plan a working schedule that allows sufficient time to develop and refine your writing.

Although writing is an idiosyncratic process, it is also a systematic one that requires careful attention to the organization and logical presentation of thoughts. The use of words that precisely describe your ideas is critical. A proposal presents a "story" that tells what you plan to accomplish and how. The major points and essential details of the story must be clearly and briefly explained.

There are several strategies that can be used to improve the quality of your proposal writing. These include organizing yourself for the task, avoiding common writing problems, and developing a grant-writing team to facilitate the process. Let's examine each strategy.

ORGANIZING FOR THE WRITING TASK

One strategy that can improve your proposal writing is to organize for the task. Box 8.1 outlines an approach you may find effective.

BOX 8.1

STRATEGY FOR ORGANIZING THE WRITING TASK

1. Set aside a block of uninterrupted time.
2. Outline the major sections of the proposal.
3. Write an initial draft without worrying about grammar.
4. Rewrite at least four to six drafts.
5. Critically evaluate your draft.
6. Ask a colleague or consultant to critically evaluate the draft.

First, set aside a block of uninterrupted time to write. Although we each have different work rhythms and styles, most people find that concentrated periods of 2 to 3 hours can be very productive. Shorter periods may not facilitate a writing flow, and efforts that are longer than 3 hours can be fatiguing. Trying to write when you are overtired can be frustrating and inefficient.

Second, start writing by outlining the major sections of the proposal. Remember, these sections should reflect either the evaluation criteria that will be used by the review panel or the specific organizing format provided by the funding agency in the application kit.

Begin to write the section with which you are most comfortable or that you feel will be the easiest to tackle first. You do not actually have to write each section in the sequence in which it will be finally presented. Writing the section with which you are most comfortable provides an immediate feeling of accomplishment and helps build momentum for the writing of other sections that may be more difficult.

Third, in the first draft you should not worry about grammar or spelling. The purpose of this draft is to capture as many ideas on paper as possible. You will have the opportunity to concentrate on the technical aspects of your writing in subsequent drafts. Nobody will have to review or evaluate this first draft, so you do not have to worry about being embarrassed by any errors you make.

Fourth, expect to write at least four to six drafts of each section. Do not expect your first drafts to be perfect. Good writing requires rewriting, rewriting, and more rewriting. You might consider adopting the 2-2-2 rule: two drafts for initial ideas, sequencing, and logic; two drafts for critical reading, idea revision, and initial editing; and two drafts for final editing and shaping.

Fifth, once you complete a satisfactory draft of a section, put it aside for a day or two. This will help you examine it from a new perspective.

In the rereading of this draft, you may discover glaring mistakes in the logic of your presentation, ideas that are not clearly represented, or gaps in the proposed design. Another approach is to read aloud a section of the proposal that is near completion. Or you can tape-record the reading and then listen carefully to how it sounds.

Another strategy is to visualize a review panel that has convened to discuss your proposal. Try to envision what a reviewer would say, especially if he or she was not familiar with your area of inquiry. These approaches all allow you to gain distance from your work and examine it from a more objective and critical perspective.

You can learn to be a critical evaluator of your own drafts, but it is also beneficial to attain the perspective of others. Obtaining constructive criticism about one's work is a difficult but important part of scholarship that can improve your scientific writing. Most writers remain too close to their work and are unable to identify gaps in logic, missing explanations, or even fatal flaws in the program design.

After you have reread and edited the draft of a particular section, or even the entire proposal, ask a colleague or pay a consultant to provide a critical, careful review. The person you choose should have some familiarity with your topic and be willing and able to appraise your work honestly. Hearing critical commentary about one's work is perhaps one of the most painful or difficult aspects of scholarship. Nevertheless, it is an important component of the process that promotes learning and intellectual growth. Do not become defensive when someone has evaluated your work as less than perfect. Instead, pay close attention to his or her reactions and comments, which are good indicators of how a review panel may receive your ideas. You can significantly improve your writing skills by studying the comments others make about your writing.

PROBLEMS WITH WRITING

The second way to improve the quality of your proposal is to avoid problems that are commonly found in writing. A major problem most people have in writing is that they do not use language in a clear and precise manner. Proposal writing is not a time to be fancy or experimental in language use and composition. A proposal requires a scientific, technical approach to writing, in which the details of your program idea are plainly explained. The proposal narrative should not be cluttered with nonessential material. Decide which details are the most important to include and incorporate them. Extraneous phrases and words make it difficult for a reviewer to understand your main points. Brevity, clarity, and organization are the keys to good proposal writing.

Listed in Box 8.2 are eight specific rules to facilitate clear writing.

1. *Stay away from jargon.* Using jargon is an imprecise approach to writing. Phrases like "meeting the needs of all patients" or "research that will address the health needs of the American

BOX 8.2

RULES FOR CLEAR WRITING

1. Stay away from jargon.
2. Avoid words that are "trendy."
3. Do not use abbreviations such as "etc."
4. Avoid colloquialisms.
5. Do not try to sound "intellectual" by using big words.
6. Avoid redundant phrases.
7. Keep overused phrases to a minimum.
8. Watch for unclear referents.

people" have very little meaning. What specific needs are you going to meet?

2. *Avoid words that are "trendy."* There are many phrases that should be used with caution in grant proposals. These include "cutting edge," "state of the art," "vis-à-vis," "in-depth," "conceptual framework," "innovative." What does the following sentence really mean: "A state-of-the-art, cutting edge, innovative conceptual framework will be developed vis-à-vis this study." If you do use words such as "innovative" or "cutting-edge," you need to explain, carefully and clearly, how or in what way the program is innovative or cutting-edge. For example, you could say, "This program is innovative in that it brings together health professionals and academic faculty to work together to develop a curriculum for students." In this way you clearly specify the aspect of the program that you consider to be innovative.

Also, do not assume that the reviewer will know the common words used in your profession. If you do use the jargon of your field, be sure to define and explain the terms carefully.

3. *Do not try to cut corners by using abbreviations such as "etc."* (e.g., women with dependent children, adolescents, teenagers, etc., commonly cited as "runaways" . . .). Using abbreviations is a lazy way of writing and reflects an inadequate development of your thoughts.

4. *Avoid colloquialisms.* You are writing a scientific proposal, so phrases such as "The findings from these studies were great!"

or "The researchers had a notion to study homelessness" are imprecise and inappropriate.

5. *Do not try to sound "intellectual."* It is not necessary to use a word with three syllables *(utilize)* when a one-syllable word *(use)* is adequate. Box 8.3 contains seven phrases that are commonly used but that can be restated to reflect an idea accurately.

6. *Avoid redundant phrases.* A point needs to be made only once. For example, phrases like "period of time," "green in color," "basic, fundamental essential," "audible to the ear," and "demographic statistical data" are examples of redundant phrases.

7. *Keep overused phrases to a minimum.* Phrases such as the following tend to be overused in proposals: "a thorough search of the literature," "an in-depth study," "a large body of information," "in the final analysis." Although the use of these phrases may be appropriate at times, they are often an indication of inadequate development of one's thoughts and are meaningless.

8. *Watch for unclear referents.* The use of unclear referents is a common problem that occurs when you begin a sentence with a pronoun that refers to someone or something in the preceding sentence. An example of an unclear reference is shown in Box 8.4. In this example, it is unclear to whom the words "they" and "their" in the second sentence refer. Do these words refer to health professionals or the homeless that are discussed in the previous sentence?

BOX 8.3

Don't use	When you can use
an excessive amount of	too much
at a high level of productivity	highly productive
at a rapid rate	rapidly
due to the fact that	because
has the capability of	can
in view of the fact that	because
serves the function of being	is

BOX 8.4

EXAMPLE OF AN UNCLEAR REFERENT

The homeless are among the most disenfranchised and underserved who could greatly benefit from the services of allied health professionals. They would contribute significantly to their health and well-being.

THE GRANT-WRITING TEAM

Another strategy to enhance the effectiveness of your proposal writing is to organize a grant-writing team. As we have said before, writing a proposal can be time-consuming and arduous. Often it is helpful to share the writing with members of a team, each of whom is assigned a specific writing responsibility. A grant-writing team enables individuals to "share the pain of writing" and to expedite the process. An added advantage of this approach is that it assigns writing responsibilities based on each member's area of knowledge and specific capability. For example, if one member of your team has an interest and expertise in curriculum development, he or she can be assigned to write the initial draft of the curriculum objectives. In a research proposal, the statistician on your team can write the statistical analysis section. In an interdisciplinary team, a literature review from each discipline can be written by the representative of that discipline.

With this approach, members of the team can be assigned roles other than writing. For example, if an individual has contact with clinical affiliates or with government agencies, he or she can be assigned to collect letters of support from those organizations.

We have found the 10 roles listed in Box 8.5 to be an effective strategy for organizing a grant-writing team. These roles organize tasks and areas of responsibility. Each member of the grant-writing team may be assigned more than one role, so it is not necessary to create a 10-member team. Three to six members is perhaps the preferred size of a grant-writing team.

1. *Proposal coordinator.* The person in this role assumes responsibility for the overall coordination of the grant-writing effort. He or she organizes the effort and assures that members complete

BOX 8.5

ROLES ON A GRANT-WRITING TEAM

1. Proposal coordinator
2. Agency contact person
3. Draft writers
4. Editor
5. Final draft writer
6. Budget coordinator
7. Coordinator of references
8. Coordinator of letters of support
9. Graphics coordinator
10. Typist and proofreader

---

their assigned tasks in a timely manner. This individual often assumes the role of principal investigator or project director on the grant application. A proposal coordinator could also serve as mentor to less experienced members of the team. In some rare instances, an individual with extensive grant-writing experience may be willing to assume the coordinator/mentor role but not serve as principal investigator.

2. *Agency contact person.* The contact person serves as liaison with the funding agency. While writing the proposal, you many need to contact the program officer to obtain feedback on the project idea, clarify the requirements of the competition, or inquire about technical matters as they emerge in the process of developing the application. Contact with the program officer should be handled by one member of the team. Usually this role is assigned to the proposal coordinator or principal investigator. However, it could also be assumed by another member of the team who is familiar with the agency or who has had previous contact with the program officer. A program officer then can associate the proposal with one person rather than several and not have to repeat advice or suggestions.

3. *Draft writers.* The first and second drafts of the proposal are usually the most difficult to write. At this stage, one or more people on the team can assume responsibility for writing an initial draft of each section. For example, a member of the team with expertise in curriculum development should be assigned the responsibility of writing the first draft of the program goals

and objectives. Other members might be more knowledgeable about research methodology or experienced at conducting literature reviews. Individuals should write the first draft of those sections for which they have the most knowledge or skill.

4. *Editor.* Either a member of the team or an outside expert should serve as an editor. An editor reads for accuracy of content and comprehensiveness as well as for grammar and punctuation, style, and format. He or she assumes the role of critic and has the responsibility of identifying gaps in conceptual development and/or unclear writing. Usually, it is best to edit for conceptual development and completeness in earlier drafts and grammar and punctuation in later drafts.

5. *Final draft writer.* Because writers have different styles, one person must take responsibility for assuring continuity in writing, particularly in the use of terminology and language style. This person should write the later drafts after all decisions about content have been made by the team. The editor or proposal coordinator often serves in this role.

6. *Budget coordinator.* One person, usually the principal investigator, should be in charge of developing the budget and obtaining the necessary institutional approvals. Once discussions have been made about the scope of the budget, it can be developed independently of the narrative sections of the proposal. Therefore, it can be completed and approved at any time and does not have to wait until the last minute.

7. *Coordinator of references.* One person can be assigned the responsibility of assuring that references are properly cited and presented in a consistent format. This is an important task that can begin as soon as an initial draft is completed. There are various computer software programs, such as Reference Manager, that are available to assist you in the organization of citations. These programs are wise investments because they provide an efficient way to complete this task.

8. *Coordinator of letters of support.* Obtaining letters of support from individuals or agencies that will be involved in your project is another important detail that can be time-consuming. This is a task that can be tackled early in the grant writing process. You should obtain letters from your congresspersons, individuals in your university or agency who can ensure institu-

tional commitment, consultants, or organizations that will be participating in your program. One member of the team can be responsible for contacting these individuals and collecting their letters.

9. *Graphics coordinator.* Using tables and graphs can effectively summarize your points and concisely organize important information. Gantt charts that describe project activities and the involvement of key personnel and figures that display the research or curriculum design are just some of the graphics you may want to include in your proposal. If you do not have a graphics software program, it is worth the price to have these materials developed by experts. Drafts of this material can be developed during the early stages of proposal writing and then revised if necessary. One member of the grant-writing team can assume responsibility for developing the initial drafts and coordinating the effort to have the materials developed.

10. *Typist and proofreader.* This is a very important role in the development of a competitive proposal. Someone who can format the final draft and proofread the proposal for consistency in presentation is an invaluable asset to a grant-writing team. Allow enough time for a secretary or administrative assistant to proofread, format, and print the final version on the correct forms.

A grant-writing team can be an effective way of organizing a submission of a proposal, particularly for those that require the participation of different disciplines or individuals with diverse areas of expertise. However, there are things to avoid and strategies to use to maximize the effectiveness of this approach. First, shared proposal writing is an effective approach to the development of initial drafts of a proposal. Because each person has a different writing style and skill level, later and final drafts should be assigned to only one or at most two individuals. This will help prevent uneven quality and other inconsistencies between sections.

Second, members of the grant-writing team must understand that the sections they contribute will be revised a number of times. It is important that participants recognize that the grant-writing process involves constant revision and modification. Knowledge of this point may prevent complaints from those team members who are sensitive to criticism about their writing or who may feel insulted when their draft is reworked.

Third, it is essential that the members of the grant-writing team complete their assigned tasks in a timely and efficient manner. The due date for a grant submission is not negotiable and the deadlines for initial drafts and other assignments should be treated similarly.

Part IV

Models for Proposal Development

Compared to other disciplines, the health and human service professions are in an initial stage of development in competing for external sources of support. This is partly due to a lack of experience in grantsmanship, a lack of available federal funds that are earmarked specifically for health professionals, and the complexity of professional life of health and human service academics and practitioners. Whereas grantsmanship is often the primary work of social and behavioral scientists, health and human service professionals must delicately balance multiple roles. These roles include training students to become practitioners, providing or administering direct services, and participating in the scientific advancement of practice. Each of these roles is time-consuming, competes for a professional's focused energies, and requires a different set of skills and expertise. Thus, the multiple roles of health and human service professionals pose a special challenge and necessitate a different, more organized approach to grantsmanship than that traditionally used in the social and medical sciences.

For this reason we believe the next two chapters are very important and provide meaningful strategies to enable professionals in both academic and practice settings to participate in the process of obtaining external funds. Chapter 9 introduces four different organizational structures for developing proposal ideas and submitting grant applications. These structures are conceptualized along a continuum from individual to collaborative team efforts. The benefits of each and the particular circumstances under which each is most effective are also discussed. Chapter 10 describes in more depth a collaborative, team approach to project development. A collaborative project structure is particularly timely in that such an approach is embedded in many funding priorities and facilitates the development of complex, multifaceted educational and research programs in health and human service. We present a model to guide the collaborative process that is based on the framework of social exchange theory and the team-building literature. The model offers a basis for bridging research and practice settings and enabling individuals from different disciplines or distinct areas of expertise to work together effectively. Knowledge of the range of organizational approaches and the collaborative process enables individuals, departments, and institutions to develop the necessary infrastructure to support grantsmanship.

Chapter 9

Four Project Structures

DESCRIPTION OF STRUCTURES

Now that you know how to identify a funding source and write a grant proposal, you can consider other important aspects of project development and implementation. The successful development and implementation of a research or educational project not only requires a knowledge of grantsmanship but also the skill to organize and manage individuals with distinct areas of expertise. Each research or training project differs in the number and complexity of its activities, the amount of coordination required, and the skills that are necessary for its participants. Therefore, to be successful, each project must be structured in such a way as to maximize organizational efficiency.

To understand the different ways of approaching the structure and management of a project, the Center for Collaborative Research in the College of Allied Health Sciences at Thomas Jefferson University examined nine research and training projects with which it was involved. On the basis of this review, four models used to organize projects were identified. These are referred to as individual, consultative, cooperative, and collaborative. Each approach has different defining characteristics, is useful under different circumstances, and has unique advantages and disadvantages. Understanding these distinct ways of approaching project development will help you develop an organizational approach that best fits your situation, project idea, and institutional setting.

The four models of project organization can be conceptualized along a continuum that ranges in degree of involvement of participants. On one end of the continuum is an individualized work effort in which there is minimal involvement of others. On the other end of the continuum is a collaborative project structure that is team oriented and requires the greatest organizational effort and level of involvement among participants. Each project structure can be defined by the extent to which 14 characteristics are present as summarized in Table 9.1. Let's examine each model.

Individual Model

An individual model reflects the "traditional" academic approach. In this model a single investigator works independently to develop and carry out a research or, in some cases, an educational project. An

TABLE 9.1   Fourteen Defining Characteristics of Project Structures

Defining characteristics	Individual	Consultative	Cooperative	Collaborative
Clear statement of goals, expectations, procedures	xxx	xxx	xxx	xxx
Differentiation of roles		x	xx	xxx
Open communication		x	x	xxx
Open, honest negotiation		xx	xx	xxx
Mutual goals			xx	xxx
Climate of trust		x	xx	xxx
Cooperation		x	xx	xxx
Shared decision making			x	xx
Conflict resolution			xx	xxx
Equality of participation				xx
Group cohesion				xx
Decision by consensus				xx
Shared leadership				xx
Shared responsibility for participation				xx

Note: x's indicate the presence of a characteristic and the level of its intensity.

individual model contains only one of the defining characteristics found in Table 9.1, that of a clear statement of goals, expectations, and procedures. Although this characteristic is a basic requirement of any project, it serves different purposes for each organizational type. For the academic, individual model, a clear statement of goals, expectations, and procedures helps an investigator remain focused and task-oriented in accomplishing the activities of the project.

An individual approach is effective and appropriate in at least five situations:

1. Small pilot grant efforts, especially those under $50,000.

2. The individual is an experienced investigator with a well-developed research agenda.

3. Competitions in which the purpose is enhancement of an individual's own career (fellowships, special training opportunities, postdoctorates, or internships).

4. The investigator is focused on a discrete piece of research, such as the structure of protein molecules in a laboratory or an investigation of the outcomes of a particular educational strategy in the classroom.

5. The investigator is the expert in all facets of a project.

An individual work model is less viable for large projects that necessitate the involvement of diverse areas of expertise and experience or require the participation of more than one organization. In fact, it is becoming increasingly more difficult for one person to have the knowledge and expertise in every facet of a project and the time to keep abreast of the literature beyond his or her field. The traditional picture of the lone researcher working in his or her laboratory developing a brilliant research project is not an effective or realistic one for the beginning investigator. Also, with the exception of those situations described above, working alone can be an isolating experience that lacks intellectual stimulation.

Consultative Model

A consultative model is an extension of the individual approach. An investigator using this model develops a project idea and then requests assistance from experts or consultants who can contribute specific skills. Consultants may be hired to write a discrete section of a proposal or perform a particular activity for a project that is funded. They do not "own" the project idea but contribute their expertise to enhance a particular aspect of it. The involvement of a consultant is usually viewed favorably by a review panel because the additional expertise increases the likelihood of the effective completion of the project.

Let's say you need to conduct a cost-effectiveness analysis in a study of a health service program but do not have that area of expertise. You would have to seek a consultant, who would be required to know only the general purposes and objectives of the program in order to work with you in determining the variables that are most appropriate to include in the analyses. He or she might have little interest in or need to understand your theoretical framework or how the program contributes to the scholarly base in your field.

A consultative model of organization has six defining characteristics: a clear statement of project goals, expectations, and procedures; differentiation of roles; open communication; open and honest negotiation; a climate of trust; and cooperation. The need for a clear statement of goals and expectations is important to help guide the overall project and identify the specific responsibilities of your consultant. Therefore, your responsibility to the consultant is to explain the project in a clear and concise fashion and describe specifically your expectations for his or her work effort.

A second characteristic, role differentiation, can be defined as a set of procedures and roles assigned to individuals to guide their behavior in carrying out specific tasks of the project. In organizing a project using a consultative model, the specific responsibilities of the consultant must be clearly communicated so that the work can be performed effectively.

Although it is important to identify a consultant with whom you can work productively, it is also important for you to solidify the working relationship through a process of open communication and negotiation. A relationship that is characterized by open communication and involves honest negotiation will help you arrive at a mutually satisfying agreement and a working climate that is productive. The relationship must also involve a level of trust and cooperation so that tasks are performed in a timely and effective manner and fit your expectations as to what must be accomplished. The agreement with the consultant should be outlined in a legally binding contract that indicates the scope of the work, the time line for its completion, and the method of payment.

A consultative model is most effective for projects in which you have adequate knowledge and skill to carry out the major activities but for which there is a need for technical expertise in a specific area. This model is appropriate for individuals in social service agencies or health care facilities, who may have knowledge in the major topic of a project but need assistance either in developing and implementing evaluation techniques or in research design. Most large projects that evolve from the ideas of an individual will require the use of one or more consultants.

Cooperative Model

A cooperative model is an extension of a consultative approach. There are two types of cooperative models. In one type, an investigator identifies an idea for a project and invites one or more individuals in the same or other disciplines at his or her institution to work on major aspects of it. The initiator of the project defines the scope of involvement of each member and directs the group's activities. A second form of this model involves a cooperative arrangement among two or more institutions. The initiating or lead institution takes overall responsibility for the conduct of the project and defines the involvement of the other institution(s) in the form of a legal contract. In both types of a cooperative structure, all parties meet to establish a systematic approach to organizing the project and to create a productive working relationship. Participants divide the project into discrete areas of responsibilities and tasks. Members of the group then meet periodically to report their progress in carrying out the responsibilities assigned to them and to make decisions about the project. Although participants work closely together, they do so as individuals, each assuming responsibility for his or her particular area. The end product of this "working group" reflects each individual's unique contribution and is an additive approach to problem solving. This cooperative, group approach is in contrast to collaborative, team approaches described in the next section, where the work product reflects an *integration* of each individual's contribution.

Cooperative models contain nine of the defining characteristics outlined in Table 9.1. As in each of the other organizational models, cooperative arrangements are based on a clear statement of goals, expectations, and procedures that defines the direction of the project and its management. In this model, role differentiation is particularly

important, because the cooperating groups must have a clear understanding of work expectations and the specific tasks that each needs
to accomplish. This working relationship requires cooperation, open
communication, honest negotiation, and professional respect or trust
if it is to be successful. The possibility of disagreement exists in any
working relationship; therefore, participating parties must also develop
an effective mechanism for making decisions and resolving conflict.

A cooperative model is effective in projects involving multiple
and distinct tasks and a clear division of labor and those in which distinct work efforts may be performed by each participating institution
or group separately. A cooperative arrangement can strengthen a project because it brings together individuals with complementary strengths
from different disciplines or institutions to carry out the project. Funding
agencies often encourage projects that are organized on this model
because it allows for meaningful contributions by many individuals or
institutions that would otherwise not be available in an individual or
consultative project structure.

Box 9.1 provides an example of a project in which a cooperative
model would be appropriate.

BOX 9.1

Dr. S., an associate professor in physical therapy, is
interested in working with young children with disabilities. She has developed a set of protocols that have
been tested and shown to be effective. Dr. S. wants to
demonstrate the effectiveness of her protocols in the
public school setting, but she does not have access to
schools nor the experience in developing training
materials that are appropriate to that setting. Dr. S.
decides to contact a colleague, Dr. T., who is a faculty
member in a school of education and has done extensive in-service work with schoolteachers. She discusses her ideas with Dr. T., who is interested in expanding
her contacts in the schools and who agrees to cooperate on the project.

As you can see in the example above, Dr. S. has specific knowledge that is useful to teachers working with children who have disabilities. However, she lacks experience with teachers and the network by
which to disseminate materials within school districts. Dr. T. has

worked extensively with schoolteachers, is familiar with public school districts, and has developed teacher training materials. Dr. S. and Dr. T. have complementary perspectives, skills, and resources. Each has access to different networks of experts, trainees, and bodies of literature, and each can accomplish a discrete work effort that addresses her own goals and areas of expertise while contributing to the accomplishment of the overall project goals. Therefore, both would benefit from a cooperative arrangement.

Collaborative Model

A collaborative model builds on a cooperative approach and involves a more complex organizational structure. Whereas cooperative models are built around working groups in which each individual contributes to the completion of a task, a collaborative model relies on the development of a "team" to work on all aspects of the project from planning to implementation. Teams are different from working groups. Working groups are based on a collection of individual actions in which performance is a function of what members do as individuals. The focus is on individual work products, with each participant accountable for the final product. In a collaborative, team-based model, there is interdependent problem solving and task performance. Successful performance requires both individual and collective actions. Collective work products reflect the joint or integrated contributions of team members, and both the individual and the group are mutually accountable (Katzenbach & Smith, 1993). Teams may be composed of health and human service professionals from the same or different disciplines, faculty members and clinicians, researchers and consumers, or any combination of these individuals.

There are many definitions of collaboration. Katzenbach and Smith (1993, p. 112) define collaboration as "a small number of people with complementary skills who are committed to a common purpose, set of performance goals, and approach for which they hold themselves mutually accountable." This definition highlights the importance of teams having "complementary skills" and a commitment to a common purpose or mutual goal.

Whitney (1990, p. 11) provides another way of understanding collaboration. She suggests that "real collaboration involves at least two different sets of ideas, known goals to be reached by each collaborator, differing and complementary talents, and a good measure of individual passion to continually generate, combine and separate activities in response to both individual and group goals." This definition emphasizes the importance of combining different ideas and the passion, energy, and commitment that is necessary to meet the challenges of the constantly changing dynamic of individuals interacting in groups.

We build on these definitions and view collaboration as "an in-depth cooperative effort in which experts from the same or different disciplines are linked in such a way that they build on each other's strengths, backgrounds, and experiences and together develop an integrative approach to resolve a research or educational problem." Thus, "problem formulation and solutions reflect a perspective that is more than the sum of each participant's contribution." (Gitlin, Lyons, & Kolodner, 1994, p. 16).

Our definition emphasizes the importance of *integrating* ideas. That is, in a collaborative effort, experts work together in such a way as to build on each other's strengths, backgrounds, and experiences, so that an integrative approach to a research, education, or training problem is achieved. Using this approach, individuals with mutual interests but perhaps different areas of expertise meet to explore potential project and proposal ideas. These individuals work closely to jointly define and develop the project idea and a plan for its implementation. Ideas for a project emerge from the interaction and exchange of individuals. Each person on a collaborative team combines his or her skills with those of other team members in such a way that problems may be redefined and solutions found that reflect multiple levels of expertise and knowledge. The final project idea and plan for implementation represents the integration of multiple perspectives and is thus the product of the group interaction. Solutions identified through this approach are much different than those that would be identified by using an additive approach to problem solving—that is, the whole is greater than the sum of its parts.

A collaborative work model contains the nine defining characteristics of a cooperative model but to a greater degree of intensity. For example, although open and honest negotiation may be present in consultative and cooperative models, this characteristic is critical for the effective development of a collaborative team. Group deliberations *must* be honest and open for a team to progress in its efforts to ascertain and integrate each member's opinion and expertise. This is not a necessary requirement for the success of a cooperative or consultative model.

A collaborative approach is also characterized by five unique characteristics: equality of participation, decision making through consensus, shared leadership, shared responsibility for participation, and group cohesion. Equality of participation is particularly important because program ideas emerge from the blending or integration of the viewpoints of all team members. All members of the team bring critical expertise to the project and therefore are essential for its effective completion. Because of the importance of these skills, each member is seen as an equal contributor to the team's deliberations. Teams that reinforce equality of participation will also seek to involve all members in decision making and recognize the value of reaching a consensus on major decisions. When members make contributions in their respective areas or expertise, they are assuming a leadership role. As individuals become more involved in decisions, they will also develop a responsibility for participation because their contributions to team decisions are seen as important to the group. These processes result in the emergence of a high level of group cohesion that, in turn, leads to an environment, or climate, of trust, in which conflicts can be openly and honestly addressed and in which members feel free to make important contributions to the grant-writing process.

The four major advantages to this organizational model are summarized in Table 9.2.

First, a collaborative approach provides an important mentoring opportunity for individuals on the team who may be less experienced in grant writing and/or conducting funded projects. Through participation and inclusion as a collaborator, an inexperienced faculty member, clinician, or service provider gains invaluable firsthand knowledge and skills. Second, a collaborative approach overcomes limited resources, such as the lack of specialized knowledge and experience, which are major barriers to grant writing in the health and human service professions. Also, the rapid advancement of scientific knowledge makes it difficult for any one person to have all the information necessary to

TABLE 9.2   Advantages of a Collaborative Model

1. Mentoring experience
2. Combining limited resources
3. Facilitating interdisciplinary interaction
4. Enabling multisite participation and development of more complex, cutting-edge projects

carry out a complex project, and many funding agencies are now encouraging interdisciplinary approaches to projects. Third, the development of a team of collaborators promotes interdisciplinary activities as opposed to the multidisciplinary participation that exists in a cooperative or consultative arrangement. Interdisciplinary collaboration allows members of one discipline to learn about and come to respect the potential contributions of those in other disciplines. This type of interaction helps to advance a particular project idea and generates respect and understanding of others from different disciplines. Finally, as in a cooperative arrangement, collaboration enables a team to develop more complex education and research projects that may involve the participation of different disciplines or multiple sites. Complex projects such as curriculum development, cost-benefit or statistical analysis, require more specialized skills that many investigators do not possess. As Katzenbach and Smith (1993) suggest, the real purpose of a collaborative team is to be "cutting edge," "revolutionizing," and "first!"

Despite the potential benefits of a collaborative approach, there are several disadvantages. First, collaboration is time-consuming in that it involves organizing and integrating the contributions of many individuals. Second, some individuals may not be able to participate in shared decision making or may not have the personality to be able to compromise and reformulate ideas. Third, collaborative projects may cost more to implement, because they involve the coordination of more individuals and necessitate frequent meetings. Finally, many academic disciplines, including those in the health and human services, are primarily concerned with their own professional advancement. This unidiscipline focus often discourages team-oriented approaches in research or education.

CHOOSING AN APPROPRIATE PROJECT STRUCTURE

The four work styles—individual, consultative, cooperative, and collaborative—offer diverse approaches to developing a project idea and a grant application. One is not necessarily better than any other. The selection of an approach depends on the nature of the idea, the complexity and size of a project, the experience of the individuals involved, and the resources available.

One way to choose the most appropriate organizational structure is to consider how much involvement of others is necessary. This can be determined by asking yourself these questions:

- Do I have the necessary skills or knowledge to carry out my idea?
- Do I have the time to complete the tasks that will be required?
- Do I have the resources needed to complete the project?

If you are lacking a specific skill, area of knowledge, time, or resources, then you should consider involving others who are capable of filling these gaps. This informal needs assessment will suggest the size and composition of your project team and the model of project organization that may be most effective.

Unfortunately, a "do it alone" attitude continues to impose a significant barrier to the health and human service professions in their efforts to advance their professions and practice through systematic inquiry. A narrow, discipline-specific approach shortchanges the professions in that problem formulation based solely in the academic environment frequently lacks relevance to daily clinical issues or results in program designs that are inappropriate for a practice setting. A uni-discipline perspective also limits the potential growth of the disciplines in that it precludes the intellectual stimulation that results from inter-actions with others.

An individual-based approach to research and education also shortchanges clinicians or practitioners who usually do not have the resources, in terms of time and research knowledge, to engage in a research or education project. Finally, the approach also shortchanges consumers. Many agencies are suggesting that it is very important to have consumers involved in the planning and implementation of programs developed by health and human service professionals. Consumers have a unique perspective and a different understanding of their own needs than do "outside experts." A productive approach for the health and human service professions is to consider a team approach that involves the equal participation of practitioners and academic faculty.

Team approaches can address many of the issues faced by health and human service professionals as they strive to improve their ability to acquire outside funding. These issues include lack of experience in grant writing, the scarcity of doctorally prepared investigators, and the lack of resources. A collaborative model has the potential to improve the skills of inexperienced faculty and practitioners and bridge the gap between the academic and clinical environments to advance research, service, and education in the health and human service fields. Although most faculty members are familiar with individual and consultative arrangements, cooperative and collaborative models may offer all professionals greater opportunities to improve their writing and project development skills.

Chapter 10

The Process of Collaboration

Recently, collaborative teamwork has received significant attention in the health and human service literature. Federal agencies and foundations have also emphasized a collaborative approach in program announcements and requests for applications (RFA). Although there is increasing interest in this approach, there are few systematic models that can be used to guide the development of collaborative teams or that describe the skills required to work effectively with others. Collaboration requires a working style that is distinct from what is needed in individual or consultative models. One must develop a team orientation to problem solving and an interdependent approach to working together and accomplishing specific tasks. For those who are used to working alone, group participation may initially be unfamiliar and difficult, appear to be too time-consuming, and seem painful. It is not surprising, therefore, that collaboration has been defined by some as "an unnatural act between two or more unconsenting adults!"

Nevertheless, as we discussed in chapter 9, under certain conditions a collaborative approach is a preferred working model and one that should be seriously considered by those in the health and human service professions. Although it may at first appear to be a cumbersome approach, it is possible to learn how to work effectively on a team and benefit from group participation. An understanding of the process of collaboration will enable you to become a more competent participant and effective leader of such an effort.

FRAMEWORK FOR UNDERSTANDING COLLABORATION

To understand the collaborative process, it is helpful to examine the way in which individuals behave in groups and how groups, in turn, shape the exchanges that occur among their members. Social exchange theory and the literature on team building are helpful frameworks for explaining the dynamics of group life. (For a discussion of the foundations of social exchange theory, see Whyte, 1943; Homans, 1961; and Blau, 1964.)

According to social exchange theory, individuals join a working group because of the perceived benefits that may be derived from membership. These benefits may be either material or nonmaterial and may include social support, opportunities for professional advancement, help in solving problems, professional advancement, and/or prestige. Groups provide opportunities for individuals to obtain these benefits but also expect certain behaviors in return, ones that will contribute to the accomplishment of the goals of the group. Thus, an interdependent relationship is formed between each member and the group as a whole. This exchange relationship is characterized as follows: Each member contributes specific skills in return for benefits provided by the group; each member brings a different skill to the group and will expect a benefit commensurate with their contributions. The group is functioning at maximum capability when these exchanges are equitable. That is, the group is effective when its goals match those of each individual, and the group can provide the desired benefits to each member in exchange for that member's skill.

In determining whether an exchange is equitable, individuals either implicitly or explicitly assess the group situation in terms of three questions (for a more extensive discussion of these questions, see Jacobs, 1970).

1. Will I obtain a given benefit if I satisfy group requirements?

2. Can I satisfy group requirements if I try?

3. Are the benefits offered worth the effort?

To answer these questions successfully, a group climate, or what we call a culture of collaboration, must exist. This culture is characterized by an environment that supports flexibility and promotes mutual trust, open communication, and cooperation. In an environment of trust and open communication, group members are able to effectively discuss their needs and what they are willing to contribute to the group in exchange for meeting these needs. The following discussion describes how these questions might be approached.

1. *Will I obtain a benefit?* One of the initial questions an individual asks himself or herself is whether there is a personal benefit for participating in a group. This question is continually asked throughout the collaborative process. In joining a group, each individual has an initial sense of what he or she expects to gain from the project (or the benefits of membership) and an idea of what he or she is willing to commit to the project in return for these benefits. Therefore, group interactions are initially characterized by a process of negotiation and renegotiation in which there is a successive series of compromises and modifications in participants' ideas, approaches to problem solving, commitments, and benefits. In these group meetings individuals refine their understanding of the benefits they hope to gain and on the basis of this understanding make a decision as to the level of commitment that will be given to the project.

2. *Can I satisfy the requirements of the group if I try?* A second important question that an individual asks is whether it is possible to carry out what the group expects. For a member of a group to feel confident about accomplishing the tasks necessary to receive the desired benefits, he or she must have a clear idea of what is expected. This requires the group and its leader to define the expectations of the project clearly so that each member knows what actions will be necessary and what the specific roles will be. Through the process of open discussion and negotiation, roles become differentiated so that members clearly understand what their responsibilities are. If each member contributes to the total group effort by doing what he or she is personally best suited to do; and if each group member has clear expectations about what the other members are going to do and how his or her own efforts fit together with theirs, not only will the skills of each individual be maximized but the members will have confidence that their efforts will not be wasted.

3. *Are the benefits offered worth the effort?* Throughout group meetings and exchanges, individuals will evaluate whether the benefits they expect to receive are worth their effort. Multiple

factors may be considered in evaluating the worth of a potential benefit. The time commitment required to obtain the benefit, one's compatibility with other group members, and the fit between one's own personal goals and those of the group are just some of the criteria used to determine the worth of the effort.

ROLES AND RESPONSIBILITIES OF TEAM MEMBERS

The team-building literature offers an understanding of the nature of the roles and responsibilities that evolve in a collaborative work effort. These roles may look and feel different from those traditionally assumed in working groups. In understanding the roles and responsibilities of team members, two concepts are helpful: role differentiation and role release.

Role Differentiation

Developing specific and clearly defined roles is a critical aspect of the collaborative group process. It is important for the group to define important roles early and to match the requirements of a particular role with the level of expertise of individual members. This process results in specialization of function and increased group stability. Groups operate more effectively when members can specialize in tasks that they can do well. Group stability is enhanced under these conditions because uncertainty is reduced when each member is clear about what is expected of them and of others. Unclear roles and poorly defined areas of responsibility ultimately lead to group conflict and dis-satisfaction of individuals. Because task requirements of the group change over time, negotiation and renegotiation as to who does what and when is a continuous process.

Despite its importance, role differentiation is difficult to achieve. Often the group leader or another member of the group may assume too much responsibility, which can be as negative as assuming too lit-tle responsibility because it can leave others in the group unsure about how to participate effectively. Obtaining just the right balance involves constant evaluation and monitoring of the group process and the roles that become differentiated.

Role Release

Another important aspect of a collaborative effort is that the specific knowledge and expertise of a role is shared with the group in such a way that others can learn the requirements of that role. This practice, which has been called role release, is very different from that which occurs in an individual or consultative model (Lyon & Lyon, 1980). In these other project structures, an individual or consultant provides expertise to solve a particular problem. However, they do not necessarily share their knowledge or teach others how to solve the problem. In a collaborative team, role release allows members to learn and develop new areas of expertise. This process increases the competence of the group and serves as a way to help individual members develop additional skills.

For example, let's say that in a collaborative effort to submit a grant application one member of the team assumes responsibility for developing a comprehensive review of the literature. This individual would be responsible for sharing how the search is conducted, the rationale for selecting specific literature, and the specific aspects of the review that are critical for all members to know and understand. In other words, this individual must release or share specific information and knowledge so that the group as a whole develops the same level of expertise. Another member's role might be to develop the budget for the project and obtain the necessary institutional approval prior to the submission of a grant application. In a role release approach, this individual would also be responsible for sharing the rationale for the budget and the specific procedural steps involved in developing and obtaining approval so that other members can gain such expertise.

Role differentiation and role release are two important components of a collaborative group structure that facilitate mentoring and professional growth. Team members with little expertise or professional experience in submitting a grant or conducting research are allowed to make a meaningful contribution to the effort through role differentiation and are taught additional skills through role release. This opportunity for growth is often perceived as an important benefit of group participation.

Potential Roles on a Team

There are a number of roles that individuals can assume on a collaborative team. The specific roles that are developed will naturally reflect the content of the grant, the scope of project-related activities, and the areas of expertise of team members.

You will probably recognize the traditional roles that individuals tend to assume on a research project as summarized in Table 10.1.

Traditionally, the principal investigator on a research grant assumes major responsibility for establishing the administrative structure, guiding the conceptualization of the project, and ensuring its scientific integrity. A project director assumes similar responsibilities for an educational program. A co-investigator is primarily responsible for more specialized areas of knowledge, such as theoretical or conceptual contributions, or supervising the implementation of a particular component of a study. The project manager, coordinator, or director is the individual who assumes responsibility for the day-to-day management of a project. This may include screening potential subjects, coordination and scheduling of interviews, supervision of interviewers, assistance in questionnaire development and management of coding and cleaning of data. Other roles listed in Table 10.1 are associated with responsibilities involved with the management of data. These include establishing and maintaining a data base for statistical analysis, cleaning raw data files, providing statistical assistance, and generating analyses.

TABLE 10.1   Roles on a Traditional Research Project Structure

Role	Responsibility
Principal investigator	Oversees entire project, especially its scientific integrity
Co-investigator	Contributes discrete area of expertise
Project coordinator/director	Day-to-date management of proposal
Interviewers	Assessment of subjects
Interventionist	Implements experimental protocol in intervention studies
Data coders/cleaners	Cleaning data, checking for accuracy of data entry
Data base manager	Establishes and maintains data files
Statistician	Assists in determining statistical manipulation

There are a number of other roles in a collaborative effort that complement the traditional project structure and facilitate the participation of individuals who may be less experienced in the research process. These roles and associated areas of responsibility are summarized in Table 10.2. This list of roles and responsibilities is not inclusive but merely suggestive of the way in which multiple tasks can be organized to match the expertise and level of experience of individual members with the requirements of the group. Each member may assume one or more roles. We have found that effective research teams have three to six participants. These roles enable individuals with different areas and levels of expertise to participate as equals on a team because equality of participation is a critical characteristic of a collaborative work effort. Matching specific roles to the area of interest and

TABLE 10.2 Roles on a Collaborative Research Team: Primary Responsibilities

Role	Project Development	Implementation
Administrative	Organizer of meetings Record keeper of project decisions	Develop codebooks Organize and maintain data records
Funding specialist	Identify funding sources Contact agencies Obtain application	Maintain contact with agency Monitor required reports
Subject specialist	Organize literature search Summarize literature	Review new literature Conduct periodic searches
Design expert	Develop design components	Monitor implementation
Statistical expert	Design statistical approach	Monitor analytic stage
Clinical site expert	Represent resources and limitations of site Design study procedures to fit site	Monitor procedures Troubleshoot problems on site Track patient census
Identify subject pool	Subject recruiter Design recruitment approach	Conduct or monitor recruitment
Data collector	Identify data collection instruments	Conduct or monitor interviews or data collection
Intervention expert	Assist in developing intervention protocol	Conduct or monitor intervention

level of expertise of each member occurs in a group meeting in which members openly discuss what must be accomplished, who will assume what responsibility, and the time frame for the completion of the task.

In addition to the roles listed in Table 10.2, one person needs to assume the role of the group leader. The group leader of a collaborative effort has a distinct role on the team that requires specific group facilitation skills. This person may be the principal investigator of a research project or the project director of a training/education grant or another individual who is appointed to coordinate the team effort because of his or her special area of expertise. The group leader must assume overall direction of the collaborative team-building effort as well as facilitate or coordinate the work tasks of the group. He or she must carefully work to orchestrate the building of an effective team in which equality of participation can emerge and in which leadership for the accomplishment of specific work efforts is shared.

Who should be a group leader? This individual should have knowledge of the grantsmanship process in addition to skill in working with groups. He or she must also be willing to commit more time and effort than other members of the team because much effort must be expended in evaluating and managing the group process inherent in team development. The group leader may be appointed by a group or may be the initiator of the team itself. Table 10.3 lists five unique responsibilities of the leader of a collaborative team effort.

TABLE 10.3   Five Group Leader/Facilitator Responsibilities

1. Ensure that each member is engaged in the group process.
2. Coordinate the work effort.
3. Guide the team through each step of the grant submission process.
4. Serve as mentor or role model as well as group participant.
5. Recognize when to direct group interactions and when to relinquish control to another team member.

FIVE-STAGE MODEL OF COLLABORATION

Now that you have a basic understanding of the processes that occur in a collaborative effort, let's examine how these processes unfold as a group develops. Based on the activities in the Department of Occupational Therapy and the Center for Collaborative Research, College of Allied Health Sciences, Thomas Jefferson University, we have developed a five-stage process model to effectively guide the development of a collaborative organizational structure. This model, which is illustrated in Figure 10.1, has been described in detail elsewhere (Gitlin et al., 1994). It was developed to bridge the gaps between health professionals, practitioners, and researchers and facilitate interdisciplinary activity in developing and implementing research and education grant programs.

This process model uses the principles of social exchange theory and the team-building literature to purposely implement a series of activities that occur in five overlapping stages. As graphically displayed in Figure 10.1, these are (1) assessment and goal setting, where key participants examine their individual and institutional goals and assess the need for developing a collaborative relationship; (2) determination of a collaborative fit, where participants discuss and negotiate project ideas and roles; (3) identification of resources and

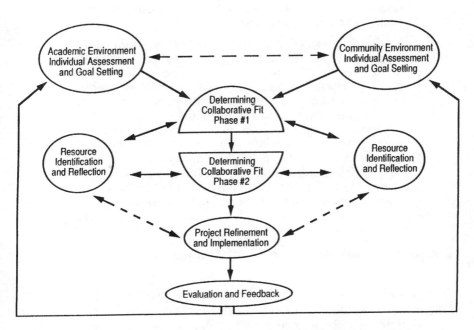

FIGURE 10.1   Five-stage model of collaboration. Adapted from Gitlin et al. (1994).

reflection, where participants return to their respective sites to reassess their resources and decide whether to participate; (4) refinement and implementation of the project, where an idea and individual roles are adjusted on the basis of the outcomes of the third stage; and (5) evaluation and feedback, where participants analyze team practices and roles and establish future goals.

Let's first consider a hypothetical situation in a typical college of allied health sciences presented in Box 10.1, to see how this model can be applied to the development of a project.

BOX 10.1

Dr. L. is an associate professor and clinical coordinator in a department of occupational therapy. In visits to rehabilitation facilities, she notices what appears to be a common theme among therapists working with older patients. The therapists express the concern that many older patients seem resistant to or unmotivated in therapeutic sessions. They question whether a better understanding of the aging process would improve their treatment approaches.

Dr. L. reviews the curriculum in her program and is surprised to learn that there is minimal content on the aging process. She mentions this to her colleague, Dr. K., in physical therapy, and finds that he has encountered a similar gap between the needs of the therapeutic community and the curriculum. Dr. L. and Dr. K. discover that Ms. G., in nursing, has the same concern. The three coordinators meet and decide to approach this problem by developing an interdisciplinary training grant involving participation of each program. They also decide that involvement of the clinical community in planning the project is critical.

Stage 1: Assessment and Goal Setting

The scenario described above describes the processes that occur in Stage 1. In Stage 1, individuals first develop an area of interest or concern that needs to be explored with others. In the above scenario, Drs. K. and L. and Ms. G., each independent of the other, identified a similar area of concern and interest in aging. Each also understood the importance of geriatric rehabilitation for their profession, department, and institution.

The second task in this stage is to identify potential collaborators. This task was easily accomplished in that the clinical coordinators knew each other and could informally discuss common concerns. In another setting, this step might involve considerable time and effort to identify potential collaborators and clinical sites.

Table 10.4 presents six self-study questions to help guide the thinking in Stage 1.

Stage 2: Determining a Collaborative Fit

Stage 2 of the model involves two phases and requires that individuals interested in participating come together in a series of meetings to determine if there is a "collaborative fit" and to establish an initial commitment to work together. The early phase of this stage involves an evaluation as to whether there are mutual goals and if individuals are committed to participation and sharing responsibility for project out-

TABLE 10.4 Self-Study Questions

1. What clinical research and/or educational issues are stimulating and important to me?
2. How do my interests and research/education ideas fit with the goals and priorities of my profession, department, and institution?
3. What expertise and resources are currently in place to develop my area of interest or specific idea?
4. What expertise and resources would be necessary to develop a project of excellence in this area?
5. What is my level of commitment in terms of time, energy, and other resources to such a project? What is the department and institutional commitment?
6. How willing am I to work with others to shape, develop, and implement this idea?
   - Am I willing to be flexible and see different sides of a question?
   - Am I willing to let go of or modify an important idea to fit the interests of others?
   - Am I willing and able to commit the time to a project?

comes. If there is agreement about the potential for collaborating in the early phase of this stage, then further discussions and negotiations can proceed. The later phase of this stage is characterized by role differentiation, a clear statement of goals and expectations, and an emerging group structure. A climate of trust will emerge if the negotiations are conducted honestly, if communication is open, if individuals cooperate with one another, and if effective conflict resolution strategies are used. If there is not a collaborative fit, then the project may be abandoned at either phase, or a decision may be made to pursue a cooperative or consultative model. Groups that effectively incorporate the viewpoints of others and develop a culture of collaboration will then proceed to Stages 3 and 4.

In the scenario presented in Box 10.1, the three clinical coordinators met to discuss their common area of concern and determine whether they would be able to work collaboratively to develop and implement a project. They also discussed their own working relationships, personal goals for the year, and time availability. Because all three had worked together on projects in the past, they were confident that they could work together on this project. They also agreed that they would keep an open mind about the direction of the project and not see it as belonging to any one discipline.

Stage 3: Resource Identification

Stage 3 activities overlap with those of Stage 2 and involve teams moving back and forth between the stages until major agreements are reached. That is, having determined that a collaborative fit is possible in Stage 2, participants must return to their respective sites or departments to reflect on the project, identify what they can contribute, and determine the individual and department advantages of participation. This resource identification and reflection is then brought back to the group for further discussion. The information may modify the group's initial plans or help refine its direction.

In the case example, the three members were able to identify resources in each of their departments, such as a curriculum emphasis on aging and previously established introductory courses. Ms. G., who did not have a doctoral degree, believed that working with more experienced team members would enhance her skills. On the basis of their independent assessments, however, they realized that they lacked knowledge of many of the day-to-day practical problems faced by clinicians and that this knowledge would be critical to a successful curriculum project. Following these discussions, each team member contacted a clinical supervisor in one of their affiliated sites, discussed their plan to write a proposal for a training grant, and asked if there was an interest in collaboration. Although each clinician was excited about the opportunity, they decided to discuss the matter with their respective department heads.

The next step for the team was to confer with their department chairpersons to see if the project was a desirable one for the department and if they could obtain release time to work on the grant proposal. Ms. G. learned that her department was expanding its undergraduate program and that this would require a significant increase in her time to coordinate student clinical experiences. Therefore, this compromised Ms. G.'s original intent to commit a large portion of her time to the development of the proposal. When she brought this information to the group for discussion, the group realized that the expansion of the nursing program actually created new opportunities for their efforts. However, they also realized that they would need to modify the original plans and role assignments to accommodate Ms. G.'s time limitations.

Stage 4: Refinement and Implementation of Project

In Stage 4 the actual work of proposal writing begins. As the writing progresses, roles may be refined and procedures redefined. It is very important in this stage to maintain open communication and deal with conflicts in an honest and straightforward manner. Proposal writing can be stressful, especially as deadlines near. Therefore, developing a climate in which people help and trust each other will lessen the effects of this stress. Although Murphy's Law, "If anything can go wrong, it will," is usually operative, the other axiom also holds, and that is, proposals always get done on time.

In our example, during Stage 4 the three faculty members met to confer about the structure of the project. They also invited representatives from the rehabilitation facilities to discuss how their organizations would be involved. As the discussion proceeded, they found that the aging process was covered in the literature of each of their disciplines but from different perspectives. This literature also suggested different approaches to dealing with the geriatric client. By learning about each other's discipline, the group was able to identify common themes. They decided to focus on these commonalities to see if, by modifying certain practices, a program could be developed that would be appropriate for all three disciplines. As these ideas evolved, they asked the clinical supervisors to evaluate the potential for success. After a series of meetings they were able to construct a model program that incorporated ideas from all three disciplines and actually went beyond what any one discipline offered. It was at this point that they realized they had developed a very close working relationship, and they began to feel more like a team than a group.

The team's next task was to determine how they would approach writing the proposal. Each discussed his or her area of strength and experience. They agreed that, as the initial idea for the project was Dr. L.'s, she would take the lead and coordinate the proposal-writing activities and have responsibility for contacting the funding agency. Dr. K. volunteered to serve as editor, especially for the final draft, and to develop the budget in collaboration with Dr. L. Ms. G. agreed to coordinate obtaining the letters of support and gathering the references. She also offered to have the secretary in her department take responsibility for final typing, formating, and developing time lines and other graphics. Each member also agreed to conduct a thorough literature search in his or her own discipline, write a draft of a section of the proposal, and request letters of support from contacts in his or her discipline.

During the negotiations and discussion of the details of the project, a number of disagreements occurred. However, Dr. L., assuming her role as team coordinator, kept bringing everyone back to points of agreement and kept checking for consensus at each point in the discussion. She also reminded everyone that it was important that all concerns about any aspect of the project be brought to the team's attention. All concerns were given a full and open hearing as the group worked toward obtaining consensus. The proposal was completed the day before the due date. During the last day each member of the team had specific responsibilities for putting the final touches on the application. For example, Dr. K. reviewed the final draft for consistency and completeness, Ms. G. supervised the duplication of the required number of copies, and Dr. L. delivered the application to the post office that evening.

Stage 5: Evaluation and Feedback

Once the proposal is completed, the entire process must be evaluated by all team members. Evaluation and feedback is an essential component of each stage of the model, as we discuss in the next section. However, Stage 5 represents a formal evaluation of the entire process by all team members. This evaluation should focus on an assessment of team functioning and include an honest reflection on the way members communicated, resolved conflicts, and made decisions. Table 10.5 presents a list of six questions to help guide this evaluation. The assessment is a very important component of a collaborative model. It not only provides an evaluation of how well the group functioned but will also prepare the team to engage in future collaborative efforts. If the proposal is funded, the group will also have the responsibility to carry out the project, and this assessment will help them improve their ability to function as a team.

In our example, the team decided to wait 2 weeks after the proposal was mailed before meeting again to assess the proposal-writing process. They believed that this period of time was long enough to allow them to "catch their breath" and yet was still close enough to the experience so that the strengths and weaknesses of the process would be fresh in everyone's mind.

TABLE 10.5   Evaluation of Team Effectiveness

1. Are there clear, cooperative goals to which every member has been committed?
2. Has there been accurate and effective communication of ideas and feelings?
3. Has there been distributed participation and leadership?
4. Are decision-making procedures appropriate and effective?
5. Do controversy and differences of opinion lead to productive solutions?
6. Is there evidence of high levels of trust, acceptance, and support among members and a high level of cohesion?

EVALUATING INDICATORS OF COLLABORATION

How do you know if your group is effectively progressing and evolving into a collaborative team? What are the indicators that a culture of collaboration is emerging? The development of teams through the use of the five-stage model involves conscious recognition of group processes and the purposeful shaping of exchanges to nurture the emergence of collaboration. At each stage of the model there are specific indicators that suggest the group is progressing effectively. These indicators are the 14 characteristics described in chapter 9. The specific stages in which they are expected to emerge are shown in Table 10.6.

Monitoring these indicators at group meetings is an important activity that can be used to facilitate the emergence of a culture of collaboration. This process may occur informally when the group leader and/or one or two other group members discuss the progress of the team. It also may occur more formally when an objective evaluator observes the group process and its outcomes, or it may occur as a combination of informal and formal techniques.

TABLE 10.6   Stage, Task, and Indicators of Effectiveness

Stage	Task	Primary Indicators of Effective Team Effort
1	Assessment and goal setting	Mutual or shared goals Clear statement of goals, expectations, and procedures
2	Determination of a collaborative fit (early phase)	Cooperation Open, honest negotiation Climate of trust established Shared decision making
2	Determination of a collaborative fit (later phase)	Open communication Role differentiation Conflict resolution
3	Resource identification and reflection	Equality of participation Shared responsibility for participation
4	Project refinement and implementation	Shared leadership Group cohesion Decision making by consensus
5	Evaluation	Three levels of assessment: individual, group, external observer

Informal Evaluation

An informal assessment merely entails reflecting on the interactions at meetings and recording the group's strengths and weaknesses. Using this approach, the leader and one or more team members briefly meet after each team meeting to evaluate the group interactions and assess them, using the 14 indicators of collaboration. It is helpful to simply record those aspects of the group meeting that represent a "green light" and a "red flag." A green light is reflected in interactions that signal that the group is ready to move ahead. A red flag is reflected in interactions that suggest some difficulties are present. For example, in Stage 1 a green light might be that all team members seem to be actively engaged in the discussion and are able to articulate specific project goals that are mutually accepted. This reflects the indicator "mutual goals." A red flag in this stage might be that some members indicate they have limited time to commit to the project or introduce conflicting approaches to developing the project. Knowledge of these green lights and red flags will help the leader structure interactions that will either move the team forward or address the potential conflict.

In conducting an informal assessment, try to identify particular behaviors or statements that illustrate a green light or that are indicative of the characteristics of collaboration for that stage. For example, by the conclusion of Stage 1 you would expect members to have generally agreed on the goals of the project and be able to articulate these clearly. Box 10.2 illustrates an interaction that reflects the emergence

BOX 10.2

Ms. K: "I am interested in pursuing a project that will advance how we assess the physical home environment. This type of assessment would enable us to provide more effective home modifications to our clients."

Dr. L: "I agree. Let's structure a project to develop an assessment tool that is of benefit to both the researcher and the health provider."

Dr. J: "This might be difficult to accomplish. We may need to consult with an expert in questionnaire design. But I agree, this should be our primary goal."

of two indicators that a collaborative relationship is forming: expression of mutual goals and clear statement of expectations and procedures.

This interaction represents a green light. That is, members seem to be committed to pursuing a joint project, and there appears to be agreement as to its nature and scope. In this case, the group leader can move the group along to the next stage of team development, which would involve discussion of the details of the project and potential funding opportunities.

Consider, on the other hand, the interaction in Box 10.3, which raises a red flag.

In this interaction the group is not ready to advance its work. Although members of the group have agreed on an area of mutual interest (delirium of the elderly in hospital settings), the way to proceed (research vs. training project) remains unresolved. This represents a basic disagreement and a potentially serious conflict. There is no evidence of a clear statement of group goals or direction at this point in the group's discussion. In this case, the group leader would need to have the group meet again to determine if this difference can be resolved. Prior to another meeting, however, the leader may assign each member a task that would help to evaluate the potential of working together. For example, one member might take the responsibility

BOX 10.3

Dr. S: "I agree that delirium is a serious problem that we often see with the elderly who enter the acute care setting. But we do not as yet know the best practices for minimizing this problem. Therefore, I suggest we focus on describing and evaluating current practices as one approach to determine what works."

Dr. M: "But this problem is so pervasive. I would like to develop training materials immediately to enable practitioners to work with the elderly more effectively."

Ms. S: "But what would these training materials include? Don't we need to first study the issue and see what is out there?"

Dr. M: "No. I disagree. That would take too long. We could develop a consensus panel to establish training materials."

for conducting a literature review of the research and training in the area of delirium. Another member might begin to identify potential funding sources in this area. The group will remain in the early phase of Stage 2 until they can reach a mutually agreeable solution.

Formal Evaluation

You might want to consider a more formal evaluative approach. Such an approach involves a systematic evaluation from three perspectives: (1) an assessment of the nature of group interactions, (2) each member's perception of his or her own behaviors in the group, and (3) each member's perception of the other members' behaviors in the group. These three perspectives provide a form of triangulation to provide an estimation of the degree of collaboration and group cohesiveness that exists.

In a formal approach, an external reviewer is hired, or one member of the group agrees to serve as an evaluator. The evaluator must remove himself or herself from group participation and remain as the objective observer of group interactions. The evaluator may want to observe and record specific behaviors that illustrate the 14 indicators of a collaborative project structure. We have developed questions to guide the identification of the 14 indicators (see Appendix C). Additionally, we recommend that the evaluator obtain appraisals from individuals at the conclusion of Stages 2 and 4. Examples of questionnaires that can be used to conduct these appraisals are also found in Appendix C.

The evaluator can provide feedback to the group by presenting the specific behaviors that are observed during group meetings, as well as the aggregated scores and responses to specific items on the self- and group-assessment questionnaires. The purpose of the feedback is to strengthen the group's team efforts by providing constructive commentary. By identifying behaviors that promote positive team performance, group members can consciously strive to model the appropriate behaviors and advance team functioning. Box 10.4 provides an example of the way feedback can be provided to a team to strengthen its efforts.

An evaluative process can also combine formal and informal approaches. Evaluation is an important reflective activity that helps each member clarify his or her own personal goals and can significantly advance the efforts of the group. Some form of evaluation must occur at each stage of the model.

BOX 10.4

EVALUATION FEEDBACK

I have observed five group meetings and have asked each member to complete two questionnaires. Let me begin by discussing my observations of the team's performance. First, it has been very exciting to see how the group's commitment to its goals have emerged over this period. This is evident in that each team member comes to the meetings on time and actively participates in the discussions. Also, there is strong evidence of respect for each member's opinion, and there appears to be equality of participation. By this I mean that each person has at one point or another taken responsibility for steering the group back on track when discussions deviate and that individuals appear to feel comfortable enough to challenge expressed opinions or at least ask for clarification.

One point I would like to emphasize is that the group has not yet differentiated roles and responsibilities sufficiently so that each member is clear as to his or her specific tasks. This is evident from the responses on the questionnaires; most members answered that they had not been assigned specific areas of responsibility and were unclear as to their specific roles. It is also evident in my own observations. For example, there appears to be confusion about the responsibilities of the group leader. On several occasions the group leader has asked for assistance in particular tasks, and no one readily volunteered. The group leader in turn has expressed feeling burdened and needing greater assistance for carrying out specific project-related activities.

I recommend that the group spend some time at this meeting to discuss each person's expectations about specific roles and responsibilities and those of the group leader. Also, the group might want to discuss a more effective way of assigning tasks. It is important to clarify roles especially at this juncture because the group needs to accomplish many tasks in a timely fashion during the next month.

PROBLEMS AND SOLUTIONS

Group work is a dynamic process that involves continual negotiation and renegotiation of goals and the roles and responsibilities of each group member. Because these efforts occur over time, groups are in a constant state of flux and change. As a consequence, a number of difficulties may emerge in the process of collaborating and as groups move through the five stages of the collaborative model. These problems may concern either individual members, the dynamics of the group interaction, or changes at the institutional level. Table 10.7 summarizes some common problems you may face while collaborating and solutions that we have found to be effective.

Individual-Based Problems

A number of difficulties related to behaviors of individuals may arise in a collaborative team effort, such as dominating discussions, interrupting other members before they have an opportunity to complete a statement, ridiculing ideas, or a negative approach to the project. These are not uncommon, especially in the beginning stage of collaboration, because some individuals are just not ready for collaboration. They may be threatened by the group process, may not endorse the goals of the group, may lack appropriate group skills, or may have a personal agenda that differs from the goals of the group. All of these behaviors cause divisiveness rather than group cohesion. The group needs to establish ground rules that ensure that divisive behaviors are not tolerated. The group leader may have to take control of meetings and redirect the group by not permitting one individual to dominate, by modeling expected behaviors, and by directly reinforcing the fact that each member's ideas are valued. The leader may also consider using a structured brainstorming session to demonstrate the advantages of team problem solving over individual solutions and emphasize that the participation of each member is valued. Box 10.5 (p. 169) describes one approach to structuring a brainstorming session.

TABLE 10.7   Common Problems and Solutions

Common Problems	Possible Solutions
Individual Members	
Divisive working behaviors that impede group work	Reexamine personal goals and team goals Restate main goals and objectives Establish ground rules for interaction Facilitate healthy disagreement
Time lines not being met	Renegotiate roles, responsibilities, and expectations Establish open communications to assure task completion Develop contingency plans
Priorities/goals of individual change	Renegotiate roles on team Expand areas of responsibility when appropriate Be prepared from outset for changes in expectations and personal goals
Group Interaction	
Conflict/differences in opinions on how to proceed	Allow all differences to be discussed State main goal and objective of the team Work through each conflicting position to see if it meets team objectives
Use of different vocabulary and way of conceptualizing an issue	Have team jointly review key articles that outline concepts Maintain dialogue about implications Ensure clarity of final decisions
Unclear goals; group seems to drift, loses sense of purpose	Keep running record of group decisions Start each meeting reviewing what has been accomplished and what remains to be done
Institution-related	
Priorities/goals of participating institution change	Prepare team for change in working environment Anticipate shifts in goals by keeping each member informed Assign members specific responsibilities that involve keeping abreast of institutional changes

BOX 10.5

WHAT IS A BRAINSTORMING SESSION?

Brainstorming is a problem-solving technique that enables a group to generate a number of ideas and think creatively. In brainstorming, each individual suspends criticism or evaluation until all ideas have been exhausted. Any idea that is presented is considered valid, and initially, the purpose is to generate as many ideas as possible.

Here are the rules to follow for one approach to structuring a brainstorming session:

Part 1: Identifying Topics or Ideas

1. The group leader states the problem area to be discussed in general terms. For example, "Our first task is to identify broad topic areas of research that we might want to pursue." Examples of broad topic areas include health promotion among culturally diverse populations, oral self-care practices among poor rural elderly, oral health of individuals with AIDS.
2. Each participant spends 5 minutes writing down a list of research topic areas or specific research questions that interest him or her.
3. Participants are then encouraged to set aside their analytic and reasoning minds and to free their spontaneous selves.
4. A basic ground rule at this stage is that any research topic or broad area for investigation is valid. This session is "freewheeling," and all ideas are accepted without any evaluative remarks (either critical or humorous).
5. One participant is appointed as the recorder and, using a flip chart or blackboard, records each idea.
6. Each participant, in order, states the first topic area on his or her sheet.
7. This process is repeated until all the ideas of each participant have been recorded.
8. Each idea is recorded in order of presentation. All ideas expressed are recorded and not screened.
9. At the end of this session the group should have generated a lengthy list of potential research areas for investigation.

Part 2: Prioritizing Ideas

1. Once the list of topics is complete, participants must begin to categorize and prioritize these ideas. The first task is to group topics into similar areas—for example, all topics that are related to community-based interventions or all topics that are related to health promotion. The second task is to prioritize each topic as either those of immediate interest or those of potential interest to all team members.

2. For those topics that are prioritized as of immediate interest, participants should discuss the specific aspects of the topic that it would be of interest to pursue. For example, members are asked to discuss the following: "What about this topic, _____, is of interest/importance?"

3. It is at this point in the session that ideas are "massaged" and evaluated and participants bring their analytic selves back to the discussion. Each idea is evaluated critically as to its feasibility in addition to its interest.

4. At the end of this session you should have three to five topic areas and specific research questions for each. However, it is important that this process not be hurried. If it becomes clear that more discussion is needed to reach agreement on the topic areas, schedule a second meeting for this discussion.

In brainstorming, each individual is given several minutes to write down a response to a problem or question that has been raised in the group. For example, let's say the group is meeting to discuss the possibility of developing a research project in home care. Individuals would first record their own thoughts about the specific topics that should be studied. After recording their thoughts, the group leader asks each member, in turn, to state one idea. This is repeated until all ideas have been shared. Each idea is written on a flip chart or board without anyone's name associated with it. In this way, each idea is given equal importance, and there is no ownership attached to it. After all ideas have been shared, the group can then problem solve about how to logically group them and critically analyze them. The group leader has a responsibility not only to ensure that the process is followed but also to monitor and prevent divisive behaviors from occurring. Therefore, brainstorming serves two purposes: it helps identify topics for investigation, and it sets a tone for the group that defines acceptable and unacceptable behavior. This activity reinforces the value of equality of participation and places equal value on each idea. Also, the group learns quickly that the list produced by the entire team is more comprehensive and sophisticated than that of any one individual.

A second problem in collaborative work that is not uncommon is a team member having difficulty in completing a task by the expected time. Other responsibilities or changes in personal priorities may take precedence for that individual. Although this may inadvertently happen to anyone, the inability to meet a deadline may have serious consequences for other members of a team, especially when a grant application must be completed by a designated date. Therefore, careful attention must be given to ensure that tasks can be and are accomplished in a timely fashion. This may include circulating to team members a written list of the tasks agreed on and the expected date of their completion, developing contingency plans for completing difficult tasks, and renegotiating the roles and areas of responsibility of individual members to ensure that all tasks can be completed. It is the responsibility of the group leader to periodically check the progress of each team member in completing these assigned tasks.

Another common occurrence in group work is that individual priorities and personal goals may change with time. Individuals may leave a group or seek different roles within it. A group needs to be prepared for shifts in the composition of the team and be ready to engage in negotiations regarding changing role responsibilities.

Group-Based Problems

The dynamics of a group itself may pose its own set of difficulties or potential barriers to team success. A natural part of group interaction is the expression of differences of opinion. These differences can be either positive or negative. On the positive side, differences of opinion stimulate thinking. They can point out inconsistencies or lack of clarity in the group's approach and, if dealt with in a positive manner, can result in the growth of ideas. On the negative side, they can be a potential source of disruption. It is important, therefore, to allow these differences to be discussed openly and to continually direct discussions toward the main goal and objective of the team.

A second potential problem is that individuals from different disciplines will enter the group with distinct work styles, a specialized vocabulary, and diverse ways of conceptualizing problems. As the group works together, it is important to build a common vocabulary and to understand how each discipline conceptualizes ideas and problems. Once this common base is developed, it allows the group to integrate the various ideas and build beyond what each discipline can contribute separately. One way to build a common foundation is to have team members read articles around common themes from each other's disciplines. This should provide all members with an understanding of the different approaches and vocabularies. Team members may also discover that a term used by one discipline may mean the same thing as a different term used by another discipline. Vocabulary and conceptual approaches should be discussed by the team to reach agreement about the common language that will be used.

Another common problem is that a group may seem to lose its sense of purpose. This may occur if discussions become redundant or when there is little to do, such as when surveys have been mailed and the group needs to wait until they are returned. To keep a team on track, a running record of group decisions and a review of these decisions at the beginning of each meeting is helpful. Another strategy is to stop meeting for a time. If there is no reason to meet, there should be no meeting. For example, if a group is meeting weekly during periods of intense activity, then, during low periods, a better use of time might be to meet less frequently, such as every 3 weeks.

Institution-Based Problems

Another potential source of difficulty impeding group performance is institution-based. For a variety of reasons, some of the priorities or goals of a department or institution may change, perhaps as a result of the appointment of a new department head or dean with a different philosophy, institutional restructuring, or changes in the external environment caused by changing economic or social conditions. Often there is very little that can be done to combat these changes. However, if the group has developed a culture of collaboration, the members will have developed a flexible attitude and should be able to accommodate these changes in their functioning. Sharing information will keep everybody informed of anticipated changes and will help prepare members for change.

Part V

Life After a Proposal Submission

Yes, there is a life after a proposal submission! After the hard work and hectic pace of submitting an application, you might not want to think about the proposal anymore, at least for awhile. That's okay because it will take some time for your proposal to be evaluated and a funding determination made.

But what does happen to your proposal when it leaves your hands? If you were to visit a federal agency in Washington, DC, on the date that grants are due, you would see the hallways cluttered with stacks of applications. Although it may appear chaotic, there is an organized process by which grant applications are categorized, assigned an identification number, and then sent out to a designated individual to be evaluated.

Knowledge of this process and how applications are reviewed can enhance the quality of your submission. Understanding the review process is an important aspect of grantsmanship and the focus of chapter 11, where we describe the grant review process, the criteria used by reviewers to evaluate applications, the potential outcomes of a review, and categories of acceptance and rejection. The biggest mistake made by new investigators is to feel so overwhelmed by a rejection that the comments of the review panel are not even read. However, there are a number of options open to you if you are not funded. These are also considered in chapter 11. It is important to recognize that few grant applications receive funding on the first submission, so consideration of and planning for a resubmission is a basic aspect of the process of grantsmanship.

Program officers often claim that just by reading proposals applicants enhance their ability to develop a competitive grant. Chapter 12 provides a case study in which we present an excerpt from a proposal and demonstrate how it would be critiqued. In addition to carefully examining chapter 12, try to arrange other opportunities for reading applications and the comments of reviewers so that you can become more skilled at developing proposals and interpreting reviewers' evaluations.

Chapter 11

Understanding the Review Process

Once you have mailed or delivered your proposal to an agency, sit back and relax. It may take 6 to 9 months, depending on the agency, to learn whether your proposal will be funded. You may wonder what happens to your proposal once it is submitted to an agency. Knowledge of the review process will enable you to understand and analyze the score you will receive and to prepare a better application if necessary. This chapter describes the review process, provides guidelines for interpreting reviewers' comments, and helps you to decide whether to resubmit your application if it is not funded. We also outline your responsibilities if you do receive funding.

STRUCTURE OF REVIEW PANELS

Each funding agency establishes its own set of procedures from which to conduct a rigorous and comprehensive review of proposals. These procedures also may differ for each competition sponsored by a particular agency. Foundations either establish special review panels for their competitions or appoint a board that assumes review responsibilities; federal agencies follow different procedures.

Let's examine the general procedures that are followed by federal agencies. If you submit a proposal to the Public Health Service (PHS), it is received by the Division of Research Grants (DRG) and assigned a number. On the basis of key words in the title or abstract of the application, your proposal is then assigned to one of several standing review panels. In the PHS system, these panels are referred to as study sections or Initial Review Groups (IRGs) and are composed of professionals with substantive knowledge and expertise in the topic area of the application. Those serving on the study sections for the National Institutes of Health (NIH) are appointed for a 3-year term based on rigorous academic and scholarly standards. There may be 15 or more individuals per study section who review applications.

The DRG will mail each reviewer a copy of the applications that have been submitted for that funding cycle. Also, the applicant will receive a postcard indicating the IRG assignment and the number the agency will use to refer to the proposal.

Other divisions of the government, such as the Bureau of Health Professions (BHPr) and Department of Education, do not have standing committees but rather appoint a group of individuals, three to five for the Department of Education and up to 10 to 15 for the BHPr, to review for a specific competition. The program officer is responsible for putting together a panel for a particular competition. This is a time-consuming process in which the program officer must select scientists who are not employed by the federal government, but who have expertise in the particular area specified for the competition. The program officer must also ensure representation from diverse geographic regions and among minority groups. Usually, only one member of an institution can serve on a review panel, and in some competitions having a panelist from the same state as an applicant is prohibited.

In most federal reviews, members are brought together to evaluate a proposal for its scientific and technical merit and to make a recommendation for funding. Reviewers typically have 4 to 8 weeks to review an average of 5 to 15 applications. The number of applications varies depending on the agency and the particular competition. Usually, proposals are sent to each panel member with very detailed instructions regarding how they are to be evaluated. In some competitions, however, reviewers do not receive the applications in advance. Instead, they must go to Washington, DC, for a week of work that involves both independent reading in a hotel room and group meetings.

A representative from the funding agency moderates or oversees the deliberations of the review panel. This representative, referred to as the executive secretary in the PHS system or as the project officer in the Department of Education, ensures that each application receives a fair and thorough review. This individual may not express a personal opinion regarding the merits of an application during the panel discussion nor assign a rating score. His or her role is to provide technical assistance, clarify agency policies, and, in some agencies, write a summary of the review for each proposal. This summary statement represents a synthesis of the deliberations of the review panel and includes a description of the proposed project, a summary of its areas of strength and weakness, a rationale for the panel's recommendation, and a numeric rating of the proposal. It is this summary, called "pink sheets" in the NIH system (because it used to be printed on pink paper), that the investigator receives whether or not the project is funded.

The agency then prepares a master list of all the applications reviewed by panels and their rankings. The summary sheets and the ranking of each application are submitted to a board that evaluates the decision for funding. In the NIH system, this board is referred to as the National Advisory Council. The council is composed of scientists and nonscientists who review each funding recommendation as to whether the proposal reflects the overall mission of the agency and provides adequate protection for human subjects. The National Advisory Council meets three times a year and makes the final decision to fund a proposal.

Before submitting a proposal be sure to inquire about the review process and the evaluation criteria that will be used. Also inquire as to whether the names of reviewers are available to the public. For example, the NIH publishes a list of members on all its standing review groups and updates this publication yearly. The Department of Education, however, releases the names of its reviewers only at the end of a funding cycle. In this case such a list is rarely helpful because it is difficult to discern the particular competition in which a reviewer participated. Occasionally, foundations will provide a list of their reviewers. Knowledge of the reviewers provides insight into the particular areas of expertise that are represented on a panel. Let's say you submit a proposal idea for which special expertise is required and this expertise is not represented by those on the existing panel. In the NIH system you may inform the DRG of the need for a specialist to be added to the review committee. For competitions in which such a request is not permissible, you would know at least know how to explain your proposal idea so that it can be easily understood by the experts who are on the review committee.

Let's look at a typical review situation.

Dr. S. is an associate professor at a major university. He agrees to serve on a Department of Education review panel that is scheduled to meet in the second week of April. Six weeks prior to the group meeting in Washington, DC, he receives eight proposals to review, for four of which he is given the responsibility of primary reviewer and for four of which he is a secondary reviewer. He also receives a detailed set of instructions and a comprehensive evaluation sheet that must be completed for each proposal. On those applications for which he is the primary reviewer, Dr. S. will write a comprehensive description and critique of the project to present during panel deliberations. He will be responsible for representing the application. For example, if a member of the review panel has a question regarding a particular procedure in the application, Dr. S. would be responsible for clarifying the issue based on his careful reading.

Dr. S. has a full teaching load, committee assignments, his own research, and commitments for presentations and manuscripts. Each proposal may need one to three careful readings to provide an adequate evaluation. To fulfill all his other obligations, Dr. S. will have to review most of the proposals in the evenings and on weekends if he expects to meet the April deadline. Obviously, Dr. S. is not going to be too happy if a proposal he is reading at 10 o'clock in the evening is difficult to read, is filled with typographical errors, or has sections missing or if he cannot find the information that fits the evaluation criteria.

As Dr. S. reviews his set of proposals, he realizes that he is currently a consultant to an institution from which he has received an application. He immediately contacts the agency to notify them of a potential conflict of interest. The agency requests that he return the application and informs Dr. S. that he will have to step out of the room during the panel deliberations for that application.

Dr. S. finishes evaluating the proposals and travels to Washington, DC, for the panel meeting. He arrives on a Sunday night and participates in an orientation session. On Monday morning, his 10-member panel meets and begins to review a total of 40 proposals. The primary reviewer for each proposal spends about 15 to 20 minutes summarizing the proposal and providing an evaluation. The secondary reviewer may spend an additional 10 minutes adding his or her comments, areas of disagreement or agreement with the primary reviewer, and evaluation. Other members of the panel, after reading the abstract and listening to the two evaluations, then spend about 20 minutes asking questions. Some may have received the application and read it prior to the meeting; others must make a judgment of merit based on the primary and secondary reviewers' presentations. As a result of this discussion, the panel decides to approve the proposal. Because this proposal was approved, the panel must then assign it a score and review the budget carefully to determine if modifications are necessary. Upon completion of this discussion, the panel members realize they have spent an hour on one proposal and have 39 more to go. Each member silently hopes that the remaining proposals will not be difficult to review so that they can make fair decisions and still get back home before their children are grown.

Obviously, the week as a peer reviewer is tiring. It highlights the need to ensure that a proposal is clearly written and follows the evaluation criteria used by panel members.

CATEGORIES OF ACCEPTANCE AND REJECTION

What are the possible outcomes of a review? Categories of acceptance and rejection vary from agency to agency. Let's first consider the system used by the PHS and then examine that of the Department of Education.

Public Health Service

Grant applications to the PHS are placed in three major categories as a result of the review process:

- "Approval"
- "Not Recommended for Further Consideration (NRFC)"
- "Defer"

Approval
Approved applications are those the IRG evaluates as having "significant and substantial scientific and technical merit." If a proposal is

approved, each member then votes a *priority rating* from 1.0 to 5.0 using the following scale:

Outstanding	1.0 – 2.0	Fair	4.0 – 5.0
Excellent	2.0 – 3.0	Marginally acceptable	5.0
Satisfactory	3.0 – 4.0		

A *priority score* is then computed by averaging the individual ratings and multiplying by 100, resulting in a priority score from 100 (highest) to 500 (lowest). Agencies that have study sections also compute a *percentile rank,* indicating the position of a priority score compared to all priority scores assigned by that IRG in its last three meetings. For example, a percentile rank of 20 means that only 20% of the applications reviewed by that study section during the last three meetings had equal or better priority scores. These two scores serve as the primary indices of scientific merit and are a major factor in determining whether an application is actually funded.

Some agencies also determine a *percentile payline,* which is a score based primarily on availability of funds. In such agencies, applications that have a percentile rank equal to or better than the percentile payline are funded. In other agencies the proposal that has the highest percentile rank is funded first. Funding proceeds with the next-highest-ranked proposals until the available money runs out. Agencies that do not compute a percentile rank fund the proposal with the highest priority score first. Investigators who are funded from the initial pool of money may be notified by letter or a telephone call.

Proposals that are approved but do not get funded are placed on a waiting list, which is arranged by percentile rank or priority score. Applications on this list may receive either full or partial funding if additional money becomes available. Approved proposals that do not make the funding cut are eligible for funding for up to 1 year. Unfortunately, after the initial distribution of funds it is rare that an approved proposal will receive funding.

Not Recommended for Further Consideration

If the IRG decides that an application does not demonstrate sufficient scientific or technical merit, it is placed in the "Not Recommended for Further Consideration (NRFC)" category. The weaknesses of such a proposal could be conceptual, scientific, or technical. In other words, your idea for the project may be inadequate or may not match the agency's priorities, the methodology may be unsound or significantly flawed, or the design may be in conflict with the rights of human subjects. This action is serious and indicates that the application will not be considered for funding in the future in its current form. Although it is possible to resubmit the proposal idea, it will have to be substantially changed, with careful consideration given to the reviewers' comments. You also should discuss your plans for revision with the project officer, who will advise you as to whether the agency will accept a future submission.

Defer

In some cases an IRG may decide that it cannot make an accurate decision about an application until additional or supplemental information is obtained. How the information is obtained depends on the nature of the competition and the information that is required. For simple issues that need clarification, such as a budget item or a missing letter of support, consortium agreement, or institutional review board approval, a project officer will contact the investigator by telephone. Substantive issues raised by a panel may need to be addressed in written form by the investigator. For example, the review panel may request clarification or additional information regarding a particular aspect of the study design. The investigator must prepare a written justification or revision of the original procedures and submit it to the project officer for final review and approval.

In some competitions, especially those involving the development of a large "center" for research or training, a site visit is made by a representative from the funding agency and either all members of the review panel or just the primary and secondary reviewers. The site visit may be for 1 to 3 days depending on the nature of the competition and the extent to which there is a need to clarify the proposed activities. During the site visit all members of the proposed project team must be present, and a formal agenda is followed. The site visitors may question the applicant on any aspect of the proposal and also examine the physical resources of the institution. Following the site visit the reviewers prepare an additional report and make a final recommendation for funding. This is evaluated by the project officer, who may also make specific suggestions as to funding and whether a substantive change in budget or procedures is necessary.

Department of Education

Funding divisions within the Department of Education follow a different set of approval procedures. Proposals are placed in two categories, "approved" and "disapproved." A proposal is rated on a scale of 0–100, based on an evaluation from three to five reviewers. Each section of a proposal has a point value attached to it. The reviewers evaluate and assign points to each section independently and then have the opportunity to revise these scores on the basis of the group discussion. An overall score for the proposal is then calculated; the overall score represents the average total score of members of the panel. Box 11.1 is an example of how one reviewer might evaluate a proposal.

Approved proposals are those that receive a panel rating of 80 or above. Those that do not are classified as disapproved. The agency funds the proposal that received the highest panel rating and continues funding proposals in descending order of their rating (all above 80) until the money runs out.

RESUBMISSION OPTIONS

Although the majority of proposals are approved, they do not receive a priority score within the funding range of an agency. The reasons for nonfunding will differ for each proposal.

BOX 11.1

Section/Criterion	Point Value	Reviewer's Score
1. Evidence of need	0–10	8
2. Relevance	0–10	8
3. Plan of operation	0–30	25
4. Nature of curriculum	0–20	18
5. Quality of personnel	0–10	9
6. Budget/cost-effectiveness	0–10	9
7. Evaluation plan	0–5	5
8. Adequacy of resources	0–5	5
TOTAL	100	87

Being rejected for funding and having to resubmit a grant is part of the process of grantsmanship. Although no one likes rejection, even the most experienced grant writer may not succeed in securing an award on the first submission of an application. Many follow the rule of "three strikes and you're out." That is, you may need to submit an application up to three times prior to receiving an award. However, given the extremely competitive nature of today's funding world and its shrinking dollars, four submissions of an application are becoming more common. If you are not funded by the fourth try, you should carefully reevaluate your proposal idea and/or its appropriateness for the agency to whom you submitted.

What are your options if you are not funded? Keep in mind that in some competitions, such as those sponsored by some foundations or those for a contract or specific request for applications (RFA), there is not always the opportunity to resubmit a nonfunded grant application. However, if it is permissible to resubmit an application, there are three steps in making a determination as to whether you should:

1. Analyzing the priority score.

2. Analyzing reviewers' comments.

3. Discussions with a project officer.

Analyzing the Priority Score

If your proposal was submitted to the PHS, you should look closely at both the priority score and the percentile rank. Both scores provide an indication of the strength of your proposal; the priority score indicates its technical or scientific merit, whereas the percentile rank compares it to other proposals evaluated by this study section. The percentile rank also provides an indication of how close you were to being funded.

For example, in the NIH system, a score of 2.5 to 3.5 implies that the proposal idea has merit but perhaps the design lacked sufficient detail. Scores in the range of 4.0 to 5.0 suggest that the reviewers may not have liked the proposal idea or the design may have had serious flaws. In such cases, major revisions are necessary before resubmitting to the next funding cycle.

Let's say you receive a score of 210 and a percentile rank of 20. If the agency funds up to 18%, then you know you were very close to being funded.

If you submitted an application to the Department of Education, you should assess both your overall score and the score from each reviewer. Let's say your score was 78. As a score of 80 is the cutoff point for the potential of funding, you know you were very close for consideration. If all three scores of the reviewers were close to 80, it indicates that the panel was consistent in judging the quality of your proposal. But the opposite may also be true. If you receive an average score of 80, this may be the result of two panel members assigning a score of 90 and one member assigning a score of 60. In this case, two panel members loved your proposal, and one had significant problems with it. The two scores of 90 would be a sign that your proposal has funding potential, but you should look at the comments of the third reviewer to understand why he or she gave you a low score. Also, carefully examine the comments of all the panelists to see if similar weaknesses were identified. If you choose to resubmit, you should pay particular attention to those issues.

Usually, proposals with scores lower than 60 indicate that the panel raised significant issues that you should examine closely. If these issues can be addressed, then a resubmission may be warranted. However, if the panel expresses lack of interest in the topic area or points out a fatal flaw in the design or a substantial issue that you cannot address, you probably should not resubmit the proposal.

Reading and Interpreting Reviewers' Comments

After receiving an official letter or telephone call informing you about the funding decision, you will obtain a copy of the reviewers' comments (the pink sheets). The format of the summary sheet varies from agency to agency. Some agencies provide an overall evaluation of your proposal and separate scores and evaluative comments made by each panel member. Other agencies provide a summary of the major strengths and weaknesses that were identified during the panel discussion. Still others will just list the major strengths and weaknesses. The pink sheets from NIH typically contain the following information:

1. A comprehensive *description* of your project and the proposed methodology.

2. A one- to three-page *critique* of each section of the proposal with particular emphasis on methods.

3. A description of the *adequacy of the investigator's* background, including publishing record and expertise to carry out the project.

4. A brief appraisal of the adequacy of the proposed *budget.*

5. A *summary* statement as to the recommendation for funding.

Regardless of the form, the comments by a review panel should be carefully evaluated because they identify the issues that must be addressed in the resubmission of the proposal.

Take a deep breath before reading the comments of the review panel. New investigators, as well as those who have received several grant awards, find it difficult to accept criticism and read the panel's deliberations. Some comments will be straightforward and will identify a particular weakness; for example, "There is no budget justification." Other comments may be less direct and open to multiple interpretations. Let's say you received the following comment: "While this appears to be an intriguing intervention, it is difficult to see how the results will significantly impact the day-to-day behavior of practicing therapists." One interpretation of this comment is that the reviewers liked the idea but did not think its significance was clearly communicated. The second interpretation is that the reviewers did not think the intervention would make a significant impact. If the first interpretation is correct, you should carefully explain the significance of the intervention for practice in your resubmission. If the second interpretation is correct, you should reexamine the intervention to see whether it is as significant as you initially believed. Sometimes it is difficult to discern which interpretation is accurate. In this case a discussion with the project officer and sharing the intervention with colleagues to elicit feedback will assist you in determining the best approach for a resubmission.

As you read and interpret the pink sheets, look for comments that say "yes" and comments that say "no" for a resubmission. Consider the examples in Box 11.2.

Panel members do try to communicate to investigators, particularly for proposals that present innovative, interesting ideas that may not be fully developed and ready for funding. On rare occasions review panels will encourage resubmissions of proposals that are disapproved. This usually occurs when the proposal contains an innovative or important idea that may not have been fully developed in the proposal.

Finally, some proposals contain what are called fatal flaws (see Box 11.3). A fatal flaw represents a fundamental problem with the

BOX 11.2

EXAMPLES OF COMMENTS THAT MAY SAY YES

1. Although this proposal has a number of weaknesses, the panel would like to urge the investigator to consider resubmission.
2. Although this proposal has a number of weaknesses, the intervention that is being tested is innovative and has the potential to make an impact on the quality of life of patients.

EXAMPLES OF COMMENTS THAT MAY SAY NO

1. Even if these changes were made, it is questionable whether this proposal could be improved sufficiently to warrant funding.
2. Although this is an interesting approach, there is some question as to its overall potential to significantly improve the delivery of services.

design or proposed program that cannot be remedied. It requires you to rethink the entire project idea and set of procedures.

Comments from a review panel can guide you in making a decision about whether to resubmit and about the kinds of changes that would be necessary to improve the proposal. You may want to share

BOX 11.3

COMMENTS THAT ILLUSTRATE A FATAL FLAW

It is apparent that this intervention would require a minimum involvement of between 8 and 10 hours per day of clinical staff time, which does not appear feasible given the staffing levels of the participating clinical sites.

This research design cannot be accomplished without random assignment of patients to experimental and control groups. It does not appear that this is possible because to do so would compromise patient treatment plans at this facility. Without random assignment, however, it is difficult to see how the study outcomes can be interpreted.

the comments or pink sheets with colleagues to obtain their reading of the panel's deliberations. Box 11.4 provides a strategy you may choose to follow for reviewing pink sheets or summary statements from the review process.

Discussions with Project Officers

It is very important to talk to the program officer who was involved with the review panel. He or she may have additional insights about the discussion that occurred among panelists. Program officers are adept at interpreting reviewers' written comments, and they may be able to provide specific suggestions to improve your proposal on the

BOX 11.4

STRATEGY FOR REVIEWING PINK SHEETS

1. Take a deep breath.
2. Read comments for general impressions and to determine if there is a fatal flaw.
3. Take another deep breath.
4. Ask a colleague familiar with your project to read the pink sheets and provide feedback.
5. Reread comments to determine:
   a. comments that say yes to resubmission
   b. comments that may say no to resubmission
   c. comments that suggest a fatal flaw.
6. List each concern or area of weakness noted by reviewers.
7. For each concern, draft a plan to address the issue.
8. If possible, share the plan with a consultant or colleague and obtain feedback.
9. Call the project officer to review your plan and obtain feedback.
10. If you resubmit, the outline of this plan can serve as the letter of introduction to your reapplication if such a letter is required.

basis of these comments. A program officer may not encourage you to resubmit if your idea does not fit agency priorities or if the review panel had problems with substantive issues in the project. Finally, if your program officer did not attend the panel discussion, he or she may encourage you to discuss specific questions of the review with the executive secretary who did sit on the study section.

The information you obtain from the questions posed in Box 11.5 is important for understanding where your application is placed in relation to the others that were submitted.

Things to Consider in a Resubmission

Let's say you finally receive notification from the agency that your proposal was approved but not funded. Your priority score was reasonably high, and the review panel did not cite any major weaknesses on the pink sheets. You call the program officer, and she confirms the panel's enthusiasm. She encourages you to revise and resubmit the proposal for the next funding cycle. You meet with your project team, and all of you decide to resubmit. What do you need to consider for a resubmission?

First, you must remember that a resubmission should be given the same careful thought as the original proposal. Do not assume that only a few editorial changes based on the suggestions of the review

BOX 11.5

WHAT TO ASK A PROGRAM OFFICER ABOUT THE REVIEW

1. How many applications were submitted?
2. How many grants were funded?
3. What were the priority scores of funded grants?
4. Given reviewer comments and score, would resubmission be recommended?
5. Will the *same* panel of reviewers evaluate a resubmission?
6. How should you indicate that the application is a resubmission?

panel are necessary. One effective strategy is to put the panel suggestions in one of three categories: major changes, minor changes, editorial changes. Major changes are those that require you to change a substantive part of the project. Examples of major changes in an educational grant are modification in the sequence or content of the courses, modification in objectives and evaluation procedures, and addition or readjustment of the overall program. In a research grant an example of a major change is a revision in the design, analytic direction, or instrument development.

Minor changes are those that require additional information that augments the proposal or statements that clarify procedures. For example, if you did not include adequate information in your statement of need for the project or a clear plan for self-sufficiency, you should gather additional information to include in these sections.

Editorial changes are those that require you to rewrite portions of a section to ensure greater clarity, to correct typographical errors, or to add figures or tables that summarize and clarify major points. Start working on the major changes first because they will require the most effort and time.

Second, remember that you need to update all materials, biographical information, funding information, and letters of support. Most agencies require that you indicate that the application represents a resubmission. Ask the program officer how best to indicate this to the review panel. Each agency has a different set of requirements for the way in which to provide such notification.

Throughout the narrative section of the proposal, highlight the substantive changes you make by either putting the section in boldface or neatly drawing a vertical line in the margin next to the section. Let the reviewers know in your summary page or cover letter how you have marked the major revisions. Some agencies require a cover letter; others request that a one-page summary be included in the body of the narrative. In the summary or letter, indicate that you carefully reviewed the recommendations by the panel and have revised and strengthened your proposal in accordance with their comments. Also, briefly outline the major changes you have made.

Depending on your interpretation of the first review you received, you may want to request that an individual with special expertise be assigned to review the resubmission. For example, let's say you proposed an ethnographic study and the panel members had expertise only in quantitative designs. You may request that an anthropologist be appointed to the review panel so that there is representation of the expertise required to review your application.

If you believe that you initially received an unfair review, you do have some recourse. You can submit a letter of complaint to your program officer or the branch chief of the agency. We should stress that this option should be used only for a glaring injustice and not because you disagree with the panel's decision. The only reason for you to write a letter like this would be to help improve the review system. You will not receive a reversal in your score or funding.

ACCEPTING AN AWARD

When you receive notification of an award (by letter or telephone), celebrate! A funded grant is a significant accomplishment and indicates that your proposal was ranked very high in comparison to the other proposals submitted to the competition.

Agencies currently must operate with very tight budgets and may be able to fund only a small percentage of proposals that are submitted in a funding cycle. In the PHS this is called the award rate, which has varied in the past 10 years from 8% to 30%. For example, an award rate of 10% means that if 200 applications are submitted, 20 awards are made.

Once you receive notification, you are in the "post-award" phase of grantsmanship. In conducting your project, there are a number of administrative details you must attend to.

Budget and Other Modifications

First, you will be notified if a revision in the budget is necessary. If it is necessary to readjust your budget, you must resubmit a revised budget for final approval. You may also be asked to revise other aspects of your program prior to the official award. Such revisions should be documented in a letter and submitted to the project officer assigned to monitor your grant.

You and the business office of your institution will receive an official notice of the award and the final approved and negotiated budget. The sponsored programs office of your institution will then establish an account from which all expenditures for the grant can be deducted. As the principal investigator or project director, you must monitor the expenditures carefully and work closely with the business office. Each institution has a set of procedures for submitting expenses and working with government grants and contracts. Make sure you know the rules and how to work effectively with the appropriate personnel.

Continued Agency Contacts

Your grant will be monitored by a project officer, either through regular telephone contact or a periodic postaward site visit. You should notify your project officer of any major or substantial changes or difficulties that occur in the process of conducting your program. For example, if you are unable to recruit the number of subjects you indicated, you should alert the officer and discuss potential strategies.

Keep in touch with your project officer. Share any manuscripts, manuals, and products that result from your efforts. Any questionnaire or product developed as part of the grant effort is legally the property of the agency. On some occasions they will share this information with other grantees.

Your project officer is a great resource from which to learn of other funded projects and may be able to provide you with the names of other professionals who are doing related activities. Also, let your project officer know when you are ready to seek additional funding. He or she will be interested in knowing how you plan to build from your current funded effort and will help you identify other potential funding opportunities.

Common Reports

Be prepared to write a report of your progress near the end of each funding cycle of your grant. Your project officer will notify you when such a report is due. This progress report represents a "noncompeting continuation grant" that is carefully reviewed by the project officer and the budget department of the granting agency. In the report you need to document your progress to date, your accomplishments, and any obstacles that have prevented you from achieving the proposed objectives. Also, and most important, submit a budget report that indicates whether there is a balance available to forward to the following year as well as a detailed proposal of the direct costs for the following year. Although you are not competing against other proposals, your record of achievement is evaluated and a decision is made as to whether the next year of your project should be funded. Therefore, the progress report must be carefully and accurately developed. After a successful review, the project officer notifies the agency's budget department to release notification of approval for continuation.

In developing next year's budget, document your direct costs. You may request only what you indicated in your initial application. A request for additional funds must be accompanied by a strong justification. For example, let's say that you or another member of the grant team has received a significant promotion that resulted in a salary increase of 10%. The original budget you developed accounted for only a 4% increase because you did not know that such a promotion would occur. If the agency has the additional funds, it may honor a request for a salary readjustment.

To facilitate the writing of the continuation report, keep an ongoing log of your major work efforts and how you achieved each objective in the first year. Keep a file of all presentations and publications so that you can easily retrieve this information. As you conduct the grant, consider the types of materials to include in an appendix. These materials may include, but are not limited to, questionnaires that have been developed, major papers, and protocols or other procedural manuals.

Also, at the end of the grant, you must write a final report that summarizes the activities to date and your significant findings or program outcomes. Usually you have 90 days after the closing of the grant period to complete such a report.

Other Administrative Considerations

As you organize your project team and begin your grant efforts, be sure to keep these other points in mind:

- In publishing your notification of award in professional newspapers or other sources, *always* indicate the funding source. Ask your project officer how to refer to the agency.
- In discussing budget issues or sending correspondence to the granting agency, always refer to the grant number that is assigned to your award by the agency.

- In presentations and/or publications resulting from your funded efforts, *always* indicate the funding source. The project officer will tell you how to make this acknowledgment.
- As the principal investigator or project director, you may be asked by the granting agency to participate on a review panel or a national meeting sponsored by the agency to discuss funded projects. These opportunities provide a mechanism by which you can share your work. They also represent a responsibility that you have to your funding agency.

Chapter 12

A Case Study

Remember Ms. L. from chapter 1? She was interested in developing an educational program to prepare an interdisciplinary group of students to work with residents of homeless shelters. Let's see what has happened to Ms. L. and her team.

If you recall, she had been advised to cast a wide net to identify external funding sources and develop a team involving other health and human service professionals. After searching for funding agencies using the sources described in chapter 2, she and her team identified 10 foundations from the *Foundation Directory* and obtained a computer printout about an inch thick from an electronic search conducted by the reference librarian. This search generated a list of a number of federal agencies and foundations that appeared interested in funding a range of programs for underserved populations. It took a few months to sift through these sources, call for more information, and request application kits, funding priorities, and a list of previously funded grants. The group then developed a concept paper to send to agencies to determine the level of interest and whether there was a potential match between the agencies priorities and the team's initial program ideas.

Finally, after 6 months of team meetings devoted to refining their ideas, reviewing literature, searching for an appropriate funding source, and visiting program officers in Washington, DC, Ms. L. and her team identified a competition and a program announcement in the *Federal Register*. The competition they identified was sponsored by the Bureau of Health Professions, Health Research Services Administration. An excerpt of this announcement is shown in Box 12.1.

The particular focus of this competition on interdisciplinary teams and programs for underserved populations motivated Ms. L. and her team to develop an application for this competition and request special consideration. To develop the application, Ms. L. and her team

BOX 12.1

EXCERPT OF AN ANNOUNCEMENT

Section 767 authorizes the Secretary to award grants to eligible entities to assist such entities in meeting the costs associated with expanding or establishing programs that will increase the number of individuals trained in allied health professions. Programs funded under this section may include:

1. those that establish community-based training programs that link academic centers to medically underserved or rural communities in order to increase the number of individuals trained;
2. those that expand or establish demonstration centers to emphasize innovative models to link allied health clinical practice, education, and research;
3. those that establish interdisciplinary training programs that promote the effectiveness of allied health practitioners in the areas of prevention and health promotion, geriatrics, long-term care, ethics and rehabilitation.

To maximize program benefit, programs that provide financial assistance in the form of of traineeships to students will not be considered for funding.

When preparing the detailed description of the Innovative Project Grant, information should be presented according to the following outline:

I.   Background and Rationale
II. Objectives

BOX 12.1 *(Continued)*

III. Project Methods
IV. Evaluation
V. Applicant Summary and Resources
VI. Budget and Justification
VII. Self-Sufficiency

Special Consideration

In determining the order of funding of approved applications, special consideration will be given to the following:

Applicants demonstrating affiliation agreements for interdisciplinary training experiences in nursing homes, hospitals, or community centers for under-served populations.

Applicants demonstrating affiliation agreements with migrant health facilities.

Funding

Approximately $1,900,000 will be available in the current fiscal year for this program. It is anticipated that approximately 10 new awards will be made, with a period of support not to exceed 3 years.

identified the roles each would assume to write the grant (as described in chapter 8) and on the project itself if it was funded.

The following section presents excerpts from the team's proposal, followed by its critique.

EXCERPT FROM A PROPOSAL

Title: *A Program to Train Interdisciplinary Health Care Teams to Work with the Homeless*

I.   Background and Rationale
      Introduction and Purpose of the Project

The departments of social work, occupational therapy, physical therapy, and nursing at the University of Excalibur propose to develop, implement, and evaluate a new program by which to educate students to provide interdisciplinary community-based health care, including health promotion and restoration services to individuals who are homeless.

This 3-year project will be accomplished in three overlapping phases: development, implementation, and evaluation. The development phase involves the formation of a partnership among social work, allied health, and nursing faculty and community leaders. The purpose of this partnership is to plan and implement a new program of didactic and clinical experiences for students in each of the programs. The implementation phase involves executing the collaboratively derived educational activities. Didactic and experiential community-based interdisciplinary training opportunities will be designed to move the student from an independent practitioner with a unidisciplinary focus to a collaborator and member of an interdisciplinary, community-based team. The evaluation phase involves appraising the success of the project. Evaluation will be conducted by the Community Advisory Board, which will assess the effectiveness of the program.

Changing Needs and Growing Numbers of Homeless

This project targets the homeless because of the demonstrated lack of health care services for this population, their clear need for both comprehensive health promotion and health restoration services, and the cost-effective role of nursing and allied health professionals in the delivery of such services. As a heterogeneous group with complex and diverse health care needs, this population challenges the present service delivery system and underscores the pressing need for community-based strategies that are effective, culturally appropriate, and comprehensive.

Who Are the Homeless?

The homeless are among the most disfranchised and underserved of the medically indigent in the United States. They are a growing, diverse population that requires creative, flexible, and holistic strategies to address their varied medical and mental health problems. Estimates of the number of homeless people vary greatly, with figures ranging from 250,000 to 350,000, based on a 1984 survey by the Department of Housing and Urban Development, to 2.5 million, as estimated by the Coalition of the Homeless in 1985. Although there is disagreement about the actual number of homeless people, there is universal agreement that their number has increased dramatically in the past several years, growing in double-digit proportion from one year to the next. Existing demographic data show consensus that the average age of the current homeless population is between 35 and 40 years, and at least one-half of the population is nonwhite. Thus, national statistics strongly support the need for the model program that is proposed in this application.

II.   Goals and Objectives
        The primary goal of the proposed program is to test an approach for developing a new community-based health care program in education, service, and research for an underserved population.
        There are three specific program objectives to accomplish this goal.
        Objective 1: Participate in yearlong activities to develop a curriculum.
        Objective 2: Expand the knowledge base and clinical abilities of faculty and community-based providers for the homeless so that they can develop and teach an innovative interdisciplinary curriculum focused on community-based health care for the homeless population.
        Objective 3: Enable faculty, in collaboration with community-based providers for the homeless, to understand and apply the linkages among theory-based practice, research, and policy formation to curriculum development.

III.   Project Methods
        The specific activities in each project phase are based on a proven learning process to develop competence in interdisciplinary team approaches. This process first involves faculty and student mastery of discipline-specific knowledge and skills in clinical decision making, clinical leadership, and health care delivery systems. Using "unidisciplinary" knowledge and skill, participants then explore potential multidisciplinary relationships. Finally, through specially designed course work in team building and practicum experiences in community-based team care, fac-

ulty and students gain competence in working on interdisciplinary community-based teams.

IV. Evaluation

The evaluation process will determine the extent to which the program represents an effective and workable model for educating students in social work, physical therapy, occupational therapy, and nursing to work on interdisciplinary community-based teams. To this end, the Project Director will charge the Consumer Advisory Board with overseeing and guiding the systematic evaluation of each phase and component of the program, with special emphasis on assessing the training curriculum. Both a formative and summative evaluation process will be developed.

V.   Budget and Justification

Project Director (Ms. L.): Ms. L. will devote 35% of her time to the project. She will direct the didactic and clinical curriculum development activities and serve as liaison with participating social service agencies and community advocates for the homeless. She will also work with each department representative to coordinate the clinical activities of each department.

Department Representatives (Dr. G., Ms. L., Dr. T.): These individuals will each devote a 10% effort and will be involved in curriculum planning, will teach specially designed courses in the program, will recruit and advise students from each of their departments, and will serve as advisors to student research projects.

Supplies: Clerical supplies, postage, telephone, and minor occupational and physical therapy equipment, such as splinting material and foam Theraband, will be required to support the operation of the project. We are requesting $3,500 during each year of the project.

Staff Travel: Travel funds in the amount of $5,200 for the first year, $5,000 during the second year, and $6,000 in the third year are being requested. Funds will be used for local travel by faculty, travel to attend three professional conferences, and travel to an international meeting in Western Europe on homelessness.

Trainee Expenses: Partial support for the 16 students in the program is requested. A stipend of $2,000/student/year is proposed.

Appendixes:

A: Letter of support from community shelter

B: Curriculum vitae of project personnel
C: Selected publications of project team

A CRITIQUE

The team's proposal arrived at the Grants Management Office of the Bureau of Health Professions. It was logged in and assigned a unique identification number. One hundred twenty proposals were received for the competition, and the program officer was very busy arranging three 10-person review panels. The reviewers each received eight proposals; for four of which they were assigned as primary reviewers and for four they served as secondary reviewers. The proposals were mailed to the reviewers 6 weeks before the scheduled panel meeting.

Ms. L.'s proposal was reviewed on the second day of deliberations. Although the proposal was well written and avoided the common writing problems identified in chapter 8, there were some fundamental issues raised by the review panel. Can you identify the issues reviewers might have had? Here is an outline of some of the strengths and weaknesses of the proposal that would have been raised by a review panel.

Strengths

1. The proposal addresses a critical need for training students to work with an underserved population.

2. The involvement of multiple disciplines and the emphasis of the program on both health promotion and restoration form an important approach.

3. The organization of three project phases represents a logical ordering of activities to accomplish the two goals of the project.

4. National data on the homeless and a strong justification of the need for services for this population are provided.

5. The project director has had extensive experience working within the shelters and organizing a volunteer program for students.

Weaknesses

1. Although the national significance of developing a program to serve the homeless is adequately demonstrated, the applicant does not provide sufficient data or information as to the local need for and benefit of this program. It is unclear whether there are any such programs existing in the applicant's region, and no needs assessment is presented.

2. The applicant proposes to develop curriculum materials based on a partnership and collaboration between community members and academic faculty. However, there is insufficient evidence of the involvement of key community members and an inadequate plan for the development of such a collaborative relationship. Such a partnership should involve members of the community in the actual planning of the grant.

3. There is only one letter of support from one of the shelters that will be involved in the program. Support letters from the other shelters and key members of the community would be advisable to ensure that this is a feasible program and acceptable to the shelters.

4. The plan for evaluation is weak and underdeveloped. Although the use of a community advisory board to assist in the evaluation is appropriate, there is no specification as to how it will evaluate the program, the criteria that will be used, or the process by which the evaluation will be carried out.

5. Objective 1 is stated as an activity, so it is difficult to determine what will be accomplished or who will participate in curriculum development.

6. There is no strong reason given for the choice of professions that will participate in the program, what important health need they will provide, or what evidence exists that they will be cost-effective. Absent from the multidisciplinary group are nutritionists, dental hygienists, educators, job placement counselors, and others who have important skills to contribute to the care and well-being of the homeless.

7. The ultimate goal of this project is unclear. Is it the provision of service to the homeless or development of an education program for students in the health professions?

8. Although the budget appears appropriate to accomplish the activities of the program, the applicant requests funds for trainee expenses. This expense is disallowed in this competition.

9. Applicant also requests funds for travel to an international meeting. Government funds cannot be used for travel outside the United States, except to Canada and Mexico.

On the basis of this review, the panel approved the proposal but assigned it a score just outside the range for funding. Thus, the review panel was sending a clear and positive message to Ms. L. and her team. This message was that the program was innovative and of great importance but needed further refinement, particularly in the plan for implementation and evaluation. Look again at each weakness that was identified. Each point can easily be addressed by Ms. L. and her team. The review panel did not identify a fatal flaw.

Although very disappointed with their score, Ms. L. and her team decided to resubmit the application. They used the reviewers' comments as a guide to develop their resubmission. The major change in their approach involved obtaining community input and identifying community leaders who would participate as members of their team. The participation of shelter directors and representatives of the homeless at the proposal development stage significantly refined the initial program idea and enabled the expanded team to obtain funding on their second submission.

Chapter 13

Common Questions and Their Answers

After reading this book, you may still have questions that are specific to your grant-writing situation. Here are 12 questions that individuals commonly ask in our grant-writing workshops or while working on a grant application with us, together with our responses. We invite other questions you may have after reading this book.

1. *How do I know if a grant is "wired" for a particular institution?* First, most competitions sponsored by government agencies and foundations are not wired or earmarked for a particular institution. Occasionally, an agency will publish a call for proposals and/or a contract that is designed for a particular institution with a special area of expertise. This occurs when the agency has a specific, focused area or question to solve for which a particular institution has both the experience and expertise to address it. However, this occurs less often than rumor would have you believe.

   One indication that a competition is wired is that the eligibility criteria are so specific that they clearly eliminate those without a previous track record or an existing program in the area. As you network among colleagues who are writing grants, you will quickly learn who has received funding and for what types of projects. This knowledge will increase your understanding of who your competitors might be in a funding competition and whether a particular request for proposals has been developed for a specific institution.

Some competitions may not be wired but may provide select institutions with a subtle advantage. For example, in developing a new program area for funding, a program officer in a foundation or federal agency may request advice and assistance from investigators with a previous record of funding in a similar area. These investigators may be asked to either comment on or suggest a direction for a new program area. Although the funding announcement that emerges from this process is not wired, it will obviously reflect the research or educational interests of those who have had input in the process and of those who have been funded. This is not to say that other investigators will not be able to develop competitive applications. However, those who have contributed to the development of the new program area will have two advantages: first, they provided input as to the types of projects to be considered for funding, and second, they would have more time to develop a competitive grant. For a more detailed discussion of how funding priorities are developed, see chapter 2.

2. *How do you "read between the lines" in a call for proposals?* There is no easy answer to this question. Reading between the lines is an ability one gains from participating in grantsmanship over the years. The best piece of advice is to read the announcement carefully and ask questions of more experienced colleagues who have worked with that agency. Learn what journals the agency prefers their funded work to be published in and the language they use to describe the area of inquiry. This will help you identify subtleties in language that will make reading between the lines easier.

3. *Why should I bother to submit an application if it is so competitive?* There is a simple answer to this question. If you choose not to submit a grant application to a competition that has relevance to your work, we guarantee that you will not be funded. If you do submit an application, you have the chance of either

being funded or, at the very least, obtaining a critical evaluation of your proposal that can be used to improve your next submission. Keep in mind that few investigators are funded on their first submission. Of course, there are some competitions that may not be appropriate, such as those that are "wired" or those that do not match your level of experience and expertise. In chapter 3 we discuss how to match your level of expertise and interests with funding agencies, and in chapter 9, we discuss different project structures and their relevance for an individual's level of experience.

4. *Are there key "buzz words" I should always use in a grant application?* You should be able to guess our answer to this question by now. No, there are no magic words or special formulas that can be applied to each grant application, except for the tips, suggestions, and knowledge you have gained by reading the preceding chapters. There are key words, however, that may be used by funding agencies to describe either the population of interest or the problem they wish to see addressed in a grant application. You can learn these terms by reading the description of the funding priority or call for proposals and the professional literature from which the priority has been developed and by reviewing projects that have been funded in previous competitions.

For example, let's say you plan to submit a grant application to the National Institute on Aging to investigate the role of "caregivers" of individuals with dementia. In the application, terms such as "caregiver," "burden," and "care recipient" could be considered appropriate buzz words because they are clearly defined in the aging literature. However, the National Institute on Disability and Rehabilitation Research (NIDRR), Department of Education, approaches caregiving from the disability perspective and labels caregivers as "personal care attendants." In writing an application to NIDRR, then, a different body of literature as well as terminology would be more appropriate. Chapter 3 discusses how to match your areas of interest and knowledge with a funding agency.

Although there are no hard-and-fast rules about words to use in all grant applications, we would suggest that you avoid jargon and terminology that is specific to your discipline. Such words are not wrong, but they will not strengthen your proposal and, in fact, might weaken it because reviewers may not understand their meaning. We discuss this issue further in chapter 8.

5. *Can I take a project officer to lunch or dinner?* The answer to this question is straightforward—*no*. Project officers are not permitted to accept gifts. This includes having their lunch, dinner, or participation in an event paid for by a constituent or potential grantee. You may have lunch or dinner with an officer but may not pick up their tab. Chapter 2 describes the questions you might discuss with a project officer.

6. *Won't a program officer think I'm a nuisance if I call him or her too often?* That depends on how often you call and what you call about. It would not be a good strategy to call a program officer once a week or any time you have a simple question. You should not take the officer's time if you can find an answer to your question elsewhere. However, program officers are public servants, and it is their job to facilitate the submission of high-quality projects. As we discussed in chapter 2, it is in the best interests of an agency to obtain as many good proposals as possible. You will also find that many program officers are scientists, who have published extensively, and are extremely knowledgeable about their own areas of inquiry. They are therefore personally committed to advancing the field and supporting quality and creative proposals.

7. *Do I need an evaluation section in my proposal, and if so, how do I develop one?* If you are developing an education or service program, most likely you will need a plan for its evaluation. There are many excellent books available and other resources on program evaluation that you can use as a guide. A traditional approach typically involves both formative and summative evaluation strategies. The specific components of your plan will depend on the objectives of the program and may involve the collection of both qualitative and quantitative information. If you are inexperienced in evaluation, consider adding a consultant to your project or collaborating with individuals in an academic institution who have such expertise. Chapters 9 and 10 discuss in more detail the project structures that include a consultative, cooperative, or collaborative relationship.

8. *Should I use a model or theory to frame the program I am developing?* A theory enables an investigator to test a set of principles and explain the outcomes of a research study. Occasionally, a call for proposals will specify that an investigator must explicitly state the theoretical framework on which an intervention or research program is based. An education or service program that is based on a theoretical model will be more competitive because such a program can be replicated and further refined and tested. Review panels recognize that the development of education, service, or research programs grounded in theory or based on testable models are important ways to advance knowledge and practice. Chapter 5 describes the sections of a grant application in more detail and where to introduce and discuss a theoretical framework most effectively.

9. *Is it unethical to pay someone, as a consultant, who has served on a review panel to give me advice about my proposal?* It is not unethical to pay someone to review your proposal. In fact, it is an excellent strategy to improve your work. Individuals who have served on review panels will have an in-depth understanding of the review process and what panel members look for in a proposal. They should also be able to identify "red flags" in your proposal. It is unethical, however, to approach someone who is currently serving on a review panel for a competition in which you have submitted a proposal. Review panel members are ethically bound not to discuss the specific proposals that are submitted.

10. *If I get rejected two or three times, does it mean I should not bother to submit again?* Not at all. Because of the increasingly competitive nature of the funding environment, it is not uncommon for someone to submit a proposal three or even four times before they are funded. A few years ago, a rule of thumb might have been "three strikes and you're out." This is no longer true. As we discussed in chapter 11, talking to a program officer and carefully reading the reviewers' comments will provide an excellent idea as to whether you should resubmit the proposal. These are better indexes of your chances than one or two rejections.

11. *What would you consider the three biggest mistakes that are made in proposals?* The biggest mistakes made in proposal writing include a failure to read the instructions, disregarding

specific topic areas that are required to be addressed in the application, and ignoring deadlines.

12. *Do I need a PhD to submit a proposal?* Legally, you do not. However, a doctoral degree is critical if you plan to be a principal investigator on a research grant because a PhD is considered a research credential. As we have discussed throughout this book, it is very important to demonstrate in the proposal that you have the qualifications to carry out a proposed project. One way to show these qualifications is through your academic credentials. However, another way to present expertise is through a track record of prior research and publication. This is one of the reasons that we have suggested the importance of a professional growth plan (chapter 3) by which to build a history of successful publications and funding. Another strategy to help overcome a lack of credentials would be to work collaboratively with others who have PhDs.

References

Blau, P. M. (1964). *Exchange and power in social life*. New York: Wiley.

Brand, M. K., Clark, N., Paavola, F. G., & Pitts, R. (1992). Strengths and weaknesses of allied health special project grant applications, *Journal of Allied Health, 21*(3), 207–218.

DePoy, E., & Gitlin, L. (1994). *Introduction to research: Multiple strategies for health and human services*. St. Louis: Mosby Year Book.

Findley, T. W. (1989). Research in physical medicine and rehabilitation. *American Journal of Physical and Medical Rehabilitation, 68*(2), 97–102.

Gitlin, L. N., Lyons, K. J., & Kolodner, E. (1994). A model to build collaborative research and education teams. *Educational Gerontology, 20,* 15–34.

Homans, G. C. (1961). *Social behavior: Its elementary forms*. New York: Harcourt, Brace and World.

Jacobs, T. O. (1970). *Leadership and exchange in formal organizations*. Alexandria, VA: Human Resources Research Organization.

Katzenbach, J. R., & Smith, D. K. (1993). The discipline of teams. *Harvard Business Review,* 111–120.

Lyon, S., & Lyon, G. (1980). Team functioning and staff development: A role release approach to providing integrated educational services for severely handicapped students. *Journal of the Association for the Severely Handicapped, 5,* 250–263.

Schumacher, D. (1994). Strategies for helping your faculty get more grants for research. *Research Management Review, 7*(1), 37–52.

Whitney, F. W. (1990). Passion and collaboration. *Nursing Connections, 3*(2), 11–15.

Whyte, W. F. (1943). *Street corner society*. Chicago: University of Chicago Press.

References

Appendix A

Key Acronyms

ACYF	Administration on Children, Youth, and Families
ADA	Americans with Disabilities Act
ADAMHA	Alcohol, Drug Abuse, and Mental Health Administration
ADD	Administration on Developmental Disabilities
AHCPR	Agency for Health Care Policy and Research
ANA	Administration for Native Americans
AoA	Administration on Aging
AOTA	American Occupational Therapy Association
APA	American Psychological Association
APTA	American Physical Therapy Association
BHPr	Bureau of Health Professions
BMCHRD	Bureau of Maternal and Child Health and Resources Development
CBD	*Commerce Business Daily*
CDBG	Community Development Block Grant
CDC	Centers for Disease Control
DADPHP	Division of Associated, Dental, and Public Health Professions
DOC	Department of Commerce
DOD	Department of Defense
DOE	Department of Energy
DOI	Department of Interior
DOJ	Department of Justice
DOL	Department of Labor
DOT	Department of Transportation
DRG	Division of Research Grants
FDA	Food and Drug Administration
FIC	Fogarty International Center
FIPSE	Fund for the Improvement of Post-Secondary Education
HIV	human immunodeficiency virus
HMO	health maintenance organization
HP/DP	health promotion/disease prevention
HRSA	Health Resources and Services Administration
HUD	Department of Housing and Urban Development
IDEA	Individuals with Disabilities Education Act

IHPO	International Health Program Office
IOM	Institute of Medicine of the National Academy of Sciences
IRB	institutional review board
IRG	initial review groups
MCH	maternal and child health
MCHB	Maternal and Child Health Bureau
NIA	National Institute on Aging
NIAAA	National Institute on Alcohol Abuse and Alcoholism
NIAID	National Institute of Allergy and Infectious Diseases
NIAMS	National Institute of Arthritis and Musculoskeletal and Skin Diseases
NICHD	National Institute of Child Health and Human Development
NIDCD	National Institute on Deafness and Other Communication Disorders
NIDDK	National Institute of Diabetes and Digestive and Kidney Diseases
NIDR	National Institute of Dental Research
NIDRR	National Institute on Disability and Rehabilitation Research
NIH	National Institutes of Health
NRFC	not recommended for future consideration
OBRA	Omnibus Budget Reconciliation Act
OSEP	Office of Special Education Programs
OSERS	Office of Special Education and Rehabilitative Services
OTs	occupational therapists
PHS	Public Health Service
RFA	request for applications
RFP	request for proposals
RO-1	designation for research projects funded by NIH
TBI	traumatic brain injury
VA	Department of Veterans Affairs

Appendix B

Sample Time Line, Budget Sheets, Flowcharts

Year ____

PHASE/ACTIVITY		SEP	OCT	NOV	DEC	JAN	FEB	MAR	APR	MAY	JUN	JUL	AUG
Phase ____	***Key Person***												
•													
•													
•													
•													
•													
•													
•													
•													
•													
•													
•													
•													
•													
•													
•													
•													

FIGURE B1 Sample time line.

PERSONNEL	SALARY SUPPORT	FRINGE BENEFITS (27.3%)	TOTAL
Project Director			
Co-Project Coordinator			
Project Secretary			
Academic Coordinator			
Clinical Coordinator			
TOTAL			
Consultants/Contracts			
Supplies			
Staff Travel			
Travel			
Other			
Indirect Costs			

TOTAL AMOUNT OF AWARD

FIGURE B2 Sample budget.

TOTAL BUDGET EFFORT

YEAR 1

Name	Total Effort	Grant Portion %	Grant Portion Amount	Institutional Portion %	Institutional Portion Amount

YEAR 2

Name	Total Effort	Grant Portion %	Grant Portion Amount	Institutional Portion %	Institutional Portion Amount

YEAR 3

Name	Total Effort	Grant Portion %	Grant Portion Amount	Institutional Portion %	Institutional Portion Amount

FIGURE B3 Total budget report.

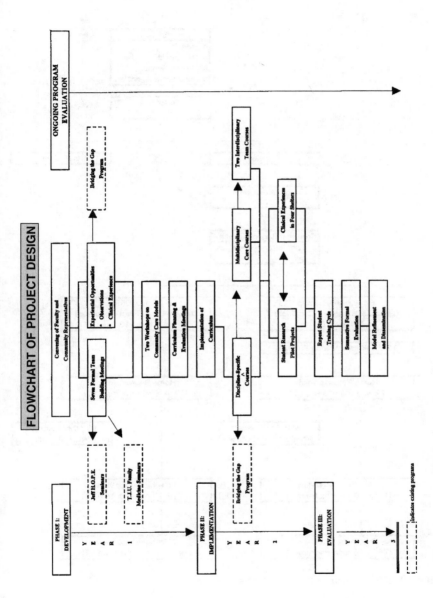

FIGURE B4   Sample flowchart.

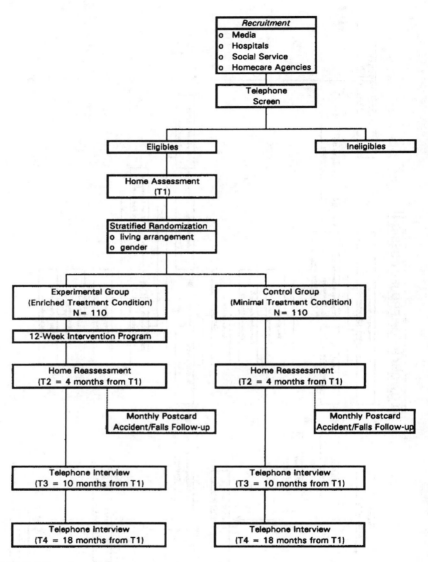

FIGURE B5   Sample flowchart of study design.

Appendix C

Guidelines for Evaluating Collaborative Teams

CHARACTERISTICS OF COLLABORATION

1. *Clear statement of goals, expectations, and procedures*

   a. Are members of the project team aware of the goals of the project?

   b. Do all members of the team fully accept the goals of the group?

   c. Does each member of the team understand his/her individual responsibilities?

   d. Does each member of the team understand the procedures that must be followed to complete the project?

2. *Role Differentiation*

   a. Does each member of the team have specified roles and responsibilities?

   b. Do team members feel responsible for accomplishing the goals of the project?

3. *Open Communication*

   a. Do members listen and pay attention to what other team members have to say?

b. Are the ideas and feelings of all members expressed openly and honestly?

4. *Open, Honest Negotiation*

a. Do team members feel free to suggest ideas for the direction of a project?

b. Are differences of opinion sought out and clarified?

c. Do team members feel free to disagree openly with each other's ideas?

5. *Mutual Goals*

a. Are team members committed to carrying out the group's task as opposed to advancing their own interests?

b. Are goals established by means of group participation?

c. Are these goals and procedures accepted by each member of the team?

6. *Climate of Trust*

a. Do team members feel free to describe their ideas, feelings, and reactions to what is taking place in the group?

   b. Do team members express acceptance and support when other members disclose their ideas, feelings, and reactions to what is currently taking place in the group?

   c. Do team members have respect, confidence, and trust in one another?

   d. Do members of the team engage in extensive and friendly interaction with one another?

7. *Cooperation*

   a. Do team members seek out opportunities to work with one another on tasks?

   b. Do team members take turns volunteering for specific tasks?

8. *Shared Decision Making*

   a. Do team members take responsibility for providing input into group decisions?

   b. Do team members have significant input into group decisions for which they have expertise?

9. *Conflict Resolution*

   a. Are disagreements brought out into the open and faced directly?

    b. When disagreements arise, do members speak freely and openly about their positions?

    c. Do members of the team feel free to disagree with others about procedures or ideas?

    d. Do team members strive to ensure that they do not change their mind about an issue just to avoid conflict and reach agreement and harmony?

10. *Equality of Participation*

    a. Does each individual, in light of his/her experience and skills, feel free to provide input to team deliberations?

    b. Is discussion distributed among all team members rather than dominated by any one perspective or person?

    c. Are the opinions of members of the teams valued by other members?

11. *Group Cohesion*

    a. Do members try to make sure others enjoy being members of the team?

    b. Do team members express acceptance and support when other members disclose their ideas, feelings, and reactions to what is currently taking place in the group?

c. Do team members try to make other members feel valued and appreciated?

d. Do team members include other members in group activities?

12. *Decision by Consensus*

a. Do team members listen to and consider other members' points of view before pressing their ideas?

b. When discussion reaches a stalemate, do team members look for the next most acceptable alternative?

c. Do team members avoid engaging in techniques such as majority rule, voting, and coin tossing to reach a decision?

d. Does the team make sure everybody accepts a solution to a problem for similar reasons?

13. *Shared Leadership*

a. Do members of the team assume responsibility for making decisions for the group related to task accomplishment?

b. Does the formal team leader facilitate discussion rather than dominate it?

   c. Are members of the team given formal responsibility for
       guiding the group to accomplish certain tasks?

14. *Shared Responsibility for Participation*

   a. Do all members of the team participate in discussions about
       important issues?

QUESTIONNAIRE ON COLLABORATION: INDIVIDUAL ROLE

The following questions are designed to gather information about your participation on [your current] project. Please respond to each honestly, using the following scale.

1 = not at all   2 = somewhat   3 = moderately   4 = very

TO WHAT EXTENT:

1. Are you familiar with the goals of this project?

   1   2   3   4

2. Do you endorse the goals of this project?

   1   2   3   4

3. Do you feel responsible for carrying out the goals of this project?

   1   2   3   4

4. Have you been assigned specific responsibilities to carry out the project?

   1   2   3   4

5. Do you understand what is expected of you?

   1   2   3   4

6. Do you understand the procedures necessary to complete the project?

   1   2   3   4

7. Do you listen to what other team members have to say?

   1   2   3   4

8. Do you feel free to express your feelings about an issue in the group?

   1   2   3   4

9. Do you express your feelings honestly about an issue in the group?

   1   2   3   4

10. Do you feel free to suggest ideas about the direction of the project?

    1   2   3   4

11. Do you feel free to disagree with other group members?

    1   2   3   4

12. Do you provide support to others when they make their ideas, feelings or reactions known?

    1   2   3   4

13. Do you have confidence in other group members?

    1   2   3   4

14. Do you volunteer for specific group tasks?

    1   2   3   4

15. Do you take responsibility to provide your expertise in group decisions?

    1   2   3   4

16. Do you value the opinions of other group members?

    1   2   3   4

17. Are you willing to assume responsibility for making a decision for the group in areas where you have expertise?

    1   2   3   4

18. Do you try to participate in group discussions?

    1   2   3   4

19. Do you feel a real part of the team?

    1   2   3   4

20. Do you feel comfortable when differences of opinion are expressed or there is conflict?

    1   2   3   4

SIMON & SCHUSTER BOOKS FOR YOUNG READERS
Simon & Schuster Building, Rockefeller Center
1230 Avenue of the Americas, New York, New York 10020
Copyright © 1991 by Juliet and Charles Snape
All rights reserved including the right of reproduction in whole or in part in any form.
Originally published in Great Britain in 1991 by Julia MacRae Books.
SIMON & SCHUSTER BOOKS FOR YOUNG READERS is a trademark of
Simon & Schuster.

Manufactured in Hong Kong.

10 9 8 7 6 5 4 3 2 1

Library of Congress Cataloging-in-Publication Data
Snape, Juliet.   Frog odyssey / Juliet & Charles Snape.   p.   cm.   Summary: When a
construction project forces the frogs to lose their pond, they venture into the city to find a
new home.   1. Frogs—Juvenile fiction.   [1. Frogs—Fiction.]   I. Snape, Charles.
II. Title.   PZ10.3.S668Fr   1992   [E]—dc20   91-12123   CIP
ISBN: 0-671-74741-X

Frog Odyssey

by Juliet & Charles Snape

Simon & Schuster Books For Young Readers

Published by Simon & Schuster

New York   London   Toronto   Sydney   Tokyo   Singapore

Albert and the frogs had lived in their pond for as long as they could remember. It wasn't the cleanest of ponds, but it was home.

One day Albert called a meeting. "We have to go," he said.
"The builders are filling up our pond."

The other frogs agreed, but Eric said, "We can't leave our favorite diving post."

"Oh, all right," said Albert. "Some of you can carry the post, and the rest can gather up the tadpoles."

Very early the next morning Albert and the frogs were ready to leave.
"Which way?" asked Nellie.
Albert sniffed the air and pointed north. "I smell water," he said.
The frogs began their journey.

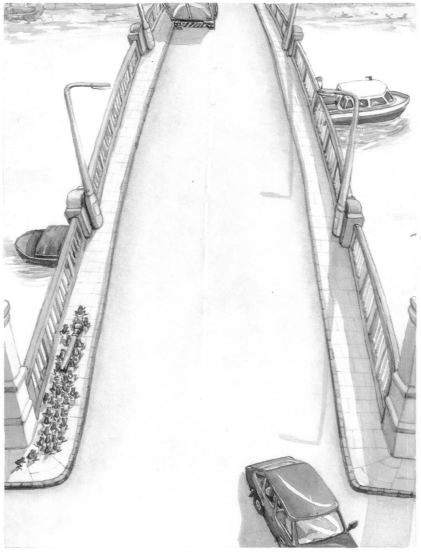

Soon they reached the river. "Can we take a dip?" asked the young frogs.

"No," said Nellie, "the river is too fast. You would all be
swept away."

"We must search further," said Albert.

On the other side of the bridge, Albert found a quiet place.
"We'll rest here for a while," he said.

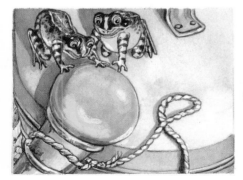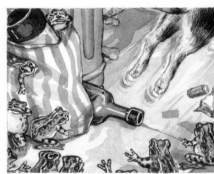

Then—DANGER! "Jump!" shouted Albert.
"YEEOOW!" shrieked the cat.
"HOORAY!" cried the frogs.

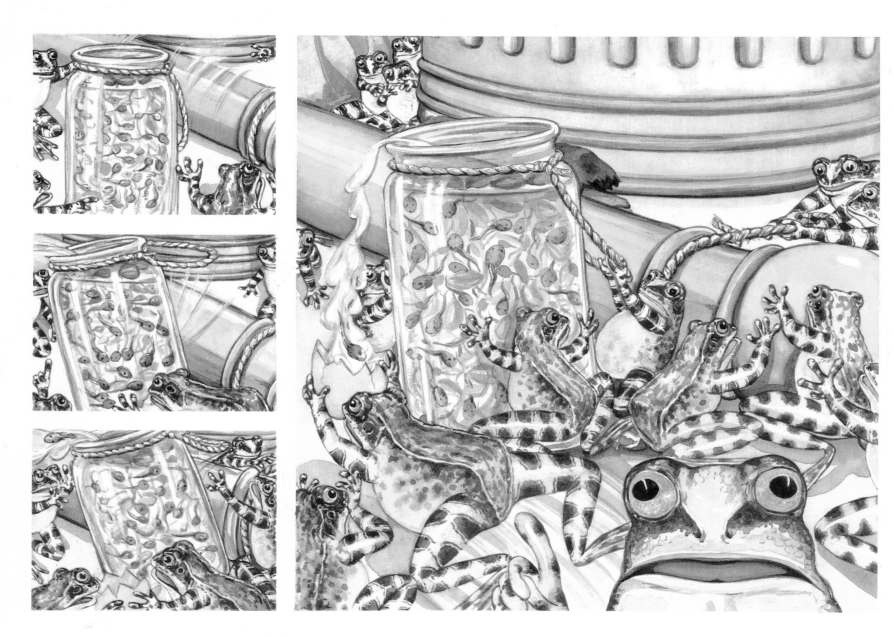

"It's not safe here," said Albert. "We must move on."
The frogs picked up the tadpole jar and the diving post.

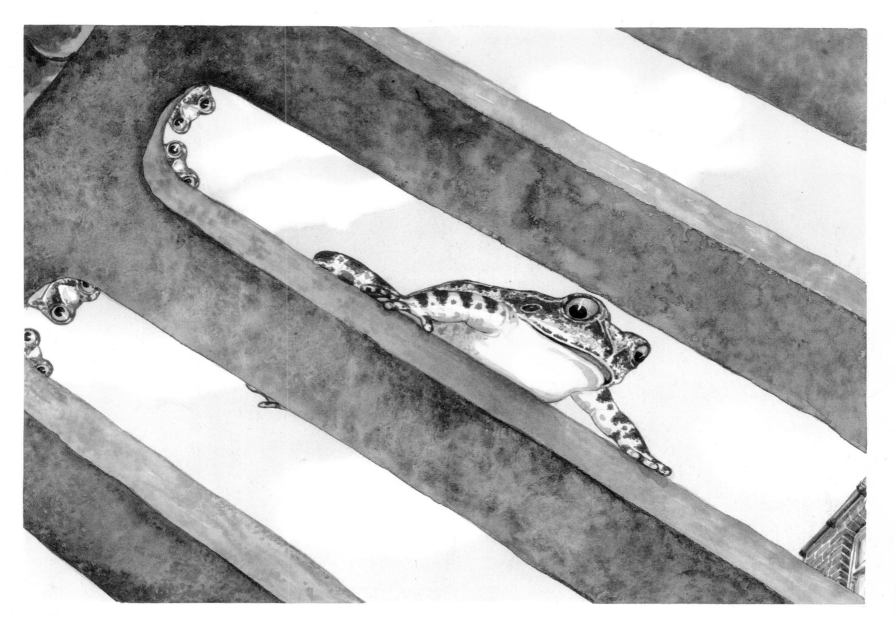

"Look over here," shouted Eric.
The frogs peered through a drain at the water rushing beneath.

"Just the place for us," said Albert, and down they all went.
They were in water again. "Isn't this wonderful?" said Albert.
"No," said Nellie. "We want a pond."
The frogs swam on.

"RATS!" cried Nellie, who was on watch at the back.
"Time to get out of here," said Albert.

The frogs saw a shaft of light and scrambled upward. Just in time, they slammed the grid down on the rats.

Albert smelled the air. "Water," he said, "let's go this way."

"Forward!" said Albert.
The frogs hopped on.

"Hop for it!" cried Nellie.

The frogs jumped on and on, until they came to a dark alley.
"Let's rest here," said Albert. "We'll look for a pond tomorrow."
The frogs huddled together and tried to sleep.

In the morning, Albert counted heads. Nellie was missing.

The streets were full of tramping feet, and the frogs didn't know which way to go. Then Eric heard something. "Look!" he cried. "It's Nellie!

"I can see trees," Nellie shouted down to them. "And WATER!"

Holding their post high, the frogs began to cross the road.
"Keep going," said Albert.

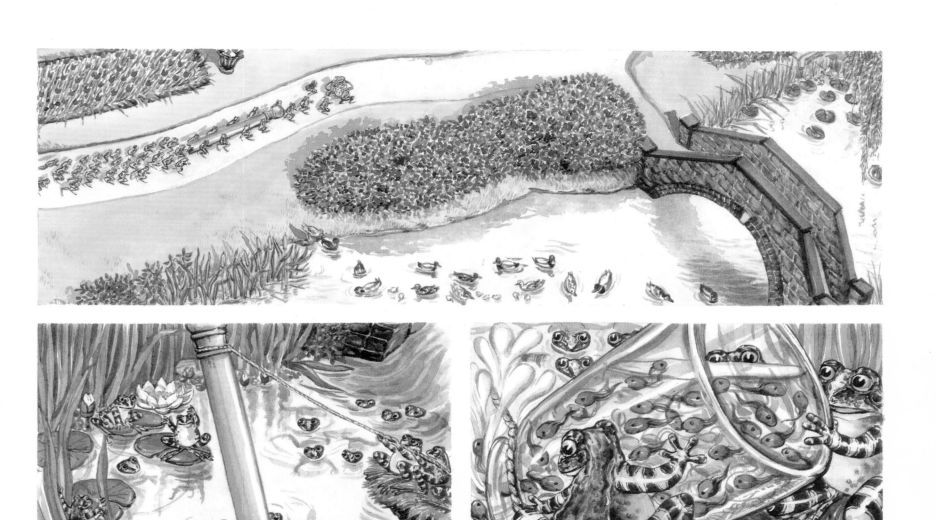

"I can smell the water," said Eric.
"And so can the tadpoles," said Nellie.
"HEAVE..." said Albert.
"HO!" said Eric.

"What a wonderful new home," said Albert.
The frogs agreed. They were happy. And so were
the tadpoles.